The Essential Guide to RF and Wireless

ISBN 0-13-025962-4

9 780130 259622

90000

Essential Guide Series

ESSENTIAL GUIDE TO TELECOMMUNICATIONS
Annabel Dodd

ESSENTIAL GUIDE TO DATA WAREHOUSING
Lou Agosto

ESSENTIAL GUIDE TO RF AND WIRELESS
Carl Weisman

The Essential Guide to RF and Wireless

CARL J. WEISMAN

Prentice Hall PTR, Upper Saddle River, NJ 07458
www.phptr.com

Library of Congress Cataloging-in-Publication Data

Weisman, Carl J.
    Essential guide to RF and wireless / Carl J. Weisman.
        p. cm. -- (Essential guide series)
    Includes bibliographical references and index.
    ISBN 0-13-025962-4
        1. Radio--Equipment and supplies. 2. Radio circuits. 3. Wireless communication systems.
    I. Title. II. Essential guide series (Prentice-Hall, Inc.)

    TK6560.W39 1999
    621.384--dc21   99-056389

Editorial/Production Supervision: *Joanne Anzalone*
Acquisitions Editor: *Bernard Goodwin*
Editorial Assistant: *Diane Spina*
Manufacturing Manager: *Alexis Heydt*
Art Director: *Gail Cocker-Bogusz*
Interior Series Design: *Meg Van Arsdale*
Cover Design: *Bruce Kenselaar*
Cover Design Direction: *Jerry Votta*

© 2000 by Prentice Hall PTR
Prentice-Hall, Inc.
Upper Saddle River, NJ 07458

Prentice Hall books are widely used by corporations and government agencies for training, marketing, and resale. The publisher offers discounts on this book when ordered in bulk quantities.
For more information, contact
    Corporate Sales Department
    Prentice Hall PTR
    One Lake Street
    Upper Saddle River, NJ 07458
    Phone: 800-382-3419; FAX: 201-236-7141
    E-mail (Internet): corpsales@prenhall.com

Printed in the United States of America

10 9 8 7 6 5 4 3 2

ISBN 0-13-025962-4

Prentice-Hall International (UK) Limited, London
Prentice-Hall of Australia Pty. Limited, Sydney
Prentice-Hall Canada Inc., Toronto
Prentice-Hall Hispanoamericana, S.A., Mexico
Prentice-Hall of India Private Limited, New Delhi
Prentice-Hall of Japan, Inc., Tokyo
Pearson Education Asia Pte. Ltd., Singapore
Editora Prentice-Hall do Brasil, Ltda., Rio de Janeiro

This book is dedicated to my parents,
Sylvan Weisman and Claire Weisman, who
taught me the joy of education and the value
of perseverance.

Contents

Part 3   RF Systems   125

Chapter 6   Older Technology   127

List of Figures

List of Tables

Preface

Nobody disputes the importance of wireless communications, and while it will surely continue to change and evolve, it is here to stay. Anybody who has received an urgent page, made an emergency call on a mobile phone, watched cable television, or been caught speeding by radar, will attest to its pervasiveness throughout everyday life. It is in recognition of the importance of RF electronics and its role in wireless communications that this book is written.

This book simplifies the subject of RF electronics with analogies, metaphors, and a minimum of mathematics. Many photographs and figures are included to further help explain the subject. Unlike other books of its kind, however, it takes a distinctly lighthearted approach to the subject by incorporating witticisms and sarcasm, occasionally directed at the book's hypothetical protagonist: the RF engineer. This book is intentionally made lighthearted because the subject matter is so dry. My feeling is, no matter how brilliantly written or factually correct an introductory book on RF is, if it is too long and boring, you will never get past the first chapter.

The Essential Guide to RF and Wireless takes an overly simplistic approach to the subject matter. In this vein, it accomplishes two main objectives: it provides a conceptual understanding of RF components and wireless systems, and it exposes you to the main vocabulary used in the industry. You can hardly expect to understand a topic as complex as wireless communications without first learning its *lingua franca*.

The Essential Guide to RF and Wireless is intended for nontechnical people who know absolutely nothing about RF, but need to or just want to explore the subject. For every engineer working in the field of RF, there are many more nontechnical people working in the field who can benefit from understanding and speaking RF. They include nontechnical managers, sales administrators, distribution specialists, manufacturer's representatives, buyers, marketing and communications personnel, advertising agents, trade show booth staffers, executive recruiters, financial analysts, and technical writers.

This book can be used in three different ways. First, it can be read cover-to-cover as the material is organized in such a way that each successive chapter builds on the one before it, starting with basic concepts and terminology, and ending with the various kinds of wireless systems. Second, each chapter can be read on a stand-alone basis, for those who need to quickly grasp a single subject or concept. Because of this stand-alone structure, some of the subject matter is repeated in an effort to make each chapter understandable by itself. Finally, this book can be used as a reference. The many tables, the Glossary, and Appendices A and B provide quick access to terminology, acronyms, and specifications used in the wireless industry.

Regardless of how you use this book, if you are new to the subject of RF, you should read all of Part 1 (Chapters 1 and 2), as the rest of the book builds on the fundamental concepts and vocabulary introduced there.

Part 2 (Chapters 3, 4, and 5) is primarily intended for those working in the RF and wireless industry, as it covers the workings of an RF system in great detail. All of the important building blocks used to make RF hardware are explained in detail, as are the different technologies used to manufacture them. Also covered is the fascinating topic of modulation, which is how ground-based information gets prepared to enter the wireless world.

Finally, Part 3 (Chapters 6 and 7) is where the fun begins. This part of the book gives you an overview of several wireless systems. Chapter 6 discusses some systems you are already familiar with, but probably never knew how they worked. Finally, Chapter 7 introduces you to the newer systems, for which the term wireless was invented. You will learn about some established wireless systems, as well as some systems that are so new they have yet to be fully deployed, or in some cases, even fully authorized.

I would like to thank one very special person, Deborah Pearson, who spent her valuable time to help me with this book. She was a tremendous source of encouragement and her effort was invaluable in proofreading the manuscript, which is quite a feat for an accountant.

If you would like to provide me with feedback on this book, feel free to contact me at weisman@flash.net.

Enjoy.

Part 1

Fundamentals

1

Basic Concepts

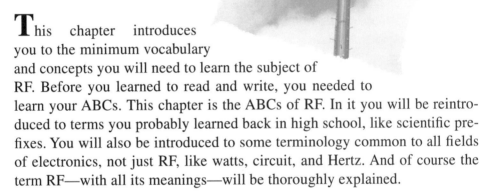

This chapter introduces you to the minimum vocabulary and concepts you will need to learn the subject of RF. Before you learned to read and write, you needed to learn your ABCs. This chapter is the ABCs of RF. In it you will be reintroduced to terms you probably learned back in high school, like scientific prefixes. You will also be introduced to some terminology common to all fields of electronics, not just RF, like watts, circuit, and Hertz. And of course the term RF—with all its meanings—will be thoroughly explained.

An important concept introduced in this chapter is the block diagram, which is a graphical depiction used to illustrate RF hardware. In this chapter it is used to show the two basic building blocks of *all* wireless systems: transmitters and receivers. The two forms which electrical energy can take are discussed, along with the two types of electrical signals: analog and digital.

Frequency, the single most important concept to understanding RF, is explained in full detail. And finally, a surprising aspect of wireless communications is highlighted—the fact that wireless communication actually involves combining two different forms of electrical energy: one to store the information and one to carry the information.

INTRODUCTION ....

WARNING! This book is an oversimplification of a very complex topic. (Your best bet is to keep it away from RF engineers.) When you are done with this book you will not be able to design RF circuits—nor should you want to. However, you should be able to converse intelligently about RF and wireless concepts, understand the lingo, and generally visualize what is going on.

The driving force behind this book is simplicity. It is meant to facilitate a qualitative understanding of an inherently quantitative topic. Many analogies and metaphors are used throughout the book to help you visualize concepts, and where there is a choice between simplicity and factual rigor, the book tends to err on the side of simplicity. My feeling is you don't need to know how to grow tomatoes to eat a pizza and you don't need to know Maxwell's equations[1] to understand RF.

This book is intended for people working in and around the RF and wireless industry without a technical degree. The assumption I have made is that you know absolutely nothing about electronics, RF, or any other arcane science. And in an effort to keep things fun, I have included only one formula for you to memorize in the entire book; here it is:

$$B = M$$

This equation means the more books which are bought, the more money I make. That's it—you can kick back and relax.

In this book the terms *RF* and *wireless* are used interchangeably just to break up the monotony. Wireless is primarily a marketing term used to describe a subset of newer, RF applications, which include things like cellular telephony and paging, to mention a few. In this book the cellular phone is frequently used as an example to help you visualize what is going on. In fact, it is beat to death. Oh well, it is simple, everyone knows what it is, and it gets the point across. Remember, the goal here is simplicity.

There are two things to note. First, this book uses block diagrams to describe RF systems. If there were another way, I would have chosen it. Unfortunately, it is the simplest way to explain what is going on. Block diagrams

---

1. Why are you looking down here? I just told you that you don't need to know it.

consist of strange symbols connected by lines in a systematic way. In some ways, block diagrams are like a foreign language which RF engineers use to communicate what is happening in their RF world. When you are done reading the book, you will be able to interpret rudimentary block diagrams. It will be like vacationing in France after listening to a Berlitz tape on French for half an hour. You'll know just enough RF to get into trouble.

Second, every attempt is made in this book to keep the subject matter fun. Heaven knows the subject matter can use it.

VOCABULARY ··

Before you begin this journey, there are a few terms with which you need to become familiar. First and foremost is the term RF. The literal meaning of RF is *Radio Frequency*. However, it is more often used in its figurative sense as both a noun and an adjective. You can generate RF (a noun) or you can generate an RF signal (an adjective). (RF can also be used to describe a range of frequencies, but more about that later.) As will be explained shortly, when used in this book, it is best to think of RF as an electrical signal which is on the move.

Prefixes

Next, you will need to know the prefixes for the powers of ten (remember chemistry?). There are only four of any consequence and they are listed in Table 1–1.

Table 1–1   Some Useful Prefixes in RF

Prefix	Meaning	Example	Interpretation
milli (m)	1/1000th	5 mW	0.005 Watts
kilo (k)	1000	3 kg	3000 grams
Mega (M)	1 million	2 MHz	2 million Hertz[a]
Giga (G)	1 billion	100 Gigabucks	Bill Gates' net worth

a. You don't know what this is yet.

Basic Electronics Terminology

Table 1–1 introduces you to another word you will need to know: watts. Watts are the unit of measure for power. If you don't know what watts are, just imagine touching a burning light bulb. A word related to power is energy, which is power times time. If a 100 watt light bulb burns for two hours, it equals 200 watt-hours of energy. If you want to envision what energy is, just imagine touching a burning light bulb for two hours. A word of caution, though—in the strange world that is RF, the words power and energy are often used interchangeably.

Two words closely related to power and energy are *voltage* and *current*. Voltage is just an electric potential, and there are two kinds: AC (alternating) voltage is the type found in a wall outlet; DC (direct) voltage is the type found in a battery. Current is simply electrons on the move. Like voltage, current can also be made either alternating or direct. The exact relationship between voltage, current, and power is simple: voltage times current equals power.

An important word related to current and voltage and one used quite often is *circuit*. A circuit is an interconnection of a bunch of electrical stuff. Electrical circuits are sometimes manufactured on something called *printed circuit boards* (PCB). If you have ever seen the inside of a computer, VCR, or any other electrical appliance, you have seen a PCB. It is just a hard, thin, plastic board with electrical stuff mounted all over it.

A word you will see occasionally is *microwaves*. It is often used interchangeably with the term RF, but is mostly used to describe a range of frequencies. *Millimeter wave(s)* is also used to describe a range of frequencies.

You have probably figured out by now that the word *frequency* is very important in the world of RF. This word will be explained in detail later, but its importance cannot be over-emphasized. If you are going to understand the concept of RF at any level, you will eventually need to grasp the concept of frequency. If you already understand what frequency is, you've got it made. If you think it has to do with how often something occurs, you're right. Stay tuned.

Since I'm going to be using the cellular phone to explain how RF things work, another word you will want to be familiar with is *basestation*. Cellular basestations consist of, among other things, those blue or gray steel towers by the side of the road which are owned by the cellular providers and are used to communicate with cellular phones.

In the world of RF, all terminology eventually gets replaced by its acronym, and so it shall be in this book. After a concept is explained and the acronym noted in parentheses, the remainder of the book will use the concept and the acronym interchangeably. Cheer up. By choosing to use acronyms, several hundred pages are eliminated from your reading. Not to worry though, Appendix A contains nothing but acronyms to help you navigate the waters.

RF BASICS ....

Transmitters and Receivers

Electrical energy moves from place to place in one of two ways. It either flows as current along a conductor (a bunch of electrons moving down a metal wire), or it travels in the air as invisible waves. In a typical wireless system, the electrical energy starts out as current flowing along a conductor, gets changed into waves traveling in the air, and then gets changed back into current flowing along a conductor again (see Figure 1–1).

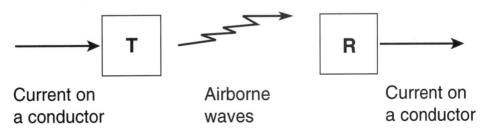

Figure 1–1   *Block diagram of a generic wireless system.*

In Figure 1–1, the electrical signal flows as current along a conductor (from the left) into the box marked "T." Inside box T, a bunch of stuff happens and out comes essentially the same electrical signal—only this time it is traveling through the air. Box T is known as the *transmitter*. It turns electrical current into airborne waves. Now traveling at the speed of light, the airborne signal reaches the box marked "R." Inside of the box marked R, some more stuff happens and out pops, you guessed it, the same electrical signal as current flowing along a conductor. Box R is known as the *receiver*. It turns airborne waves into electrical current.

Sometimes RF engineers combine a transmitter and a receiver into a single functioning unit. Now what do you suppose they call this ingenious amalgam? A *transceiver.*

Signals

Analog Signals

Electrical energy (either current or waves) can actually store information if it is made to vary (in intensity) over time. When electrical energy varies over time in a controlled manner it is called a *signal*. Signals fall into one of two general categories: *analog* or *digital*. For those of you who were unfortunate enough to have suffered through high school trigonometry, you probably remember the sine wave. At the risk of stirring up horrible memories, there is a sine wave shown in Figure 1–2. As time goes by (moving from left to right in Figure 1–2), the intensity of a sine wave grows to some maximum at point B, then back to zero at point C, and on to some minimum value at point D, before finally returning to zero at point E and starting the whole process all over again and again and again.

A sine wave is an example of an analog signal. Whether it is current flowing down a wire or a wave traveling in the air, a sine wave signal varies (in intensity) exactly as shown in Figure 1–2. In the RF world, the intensity of a signal is almost always a measure of power (remember watts?). The number of times a signal goes through a complete up and down cycle (from point A to point E) in one second is the signal's *frequency* (measured in Hertz[2] and abbreviated Hz). If you find it difficult to remember what Hertz means, every time you hear the word Hertz just replace it with the term "cycles per second." To get an appreciation for how fast these signals go up and down, a 900 MHz (megahertz) signal utilized in cellular telephony, not a particularly high frequency by today's standards, exhibits 900 *million* ups and downs in a single second. Wow!

---

2. Now you know what this is.

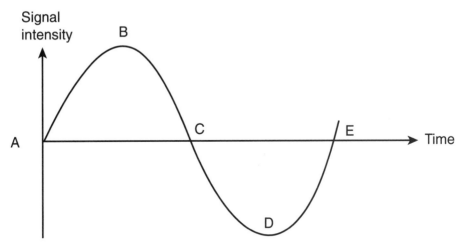

Figure 1–2   A sine wave.

Frequency

As mentioned in the introduction, the concept of frequency is key to understanding RF, because all RF stuff is frequency-dependent. That is, it can distinguish between two different signals *solely* on the basis of their different frequencies. Frequency is what separates one RF signal from another and it is what distinguishes one wireless application from another. Table 1–2 contains a sample of different wireless activities at different frequencies. You may not know what they all are yet, but you can still observe two things. First, notice how many different frequency-dependent applications there are—this is just a small sample—and second, the table is organized in such a way as to give you an appreciation for the difference in magnitude of all the frequencies.

Table 1–2   The Frequency of Various Activities

Frequency in Hertz	Application
60	Electrical wall outlet
2,000	The human voice
530,000	AM radio
54,000,000	TV channel 2 (VHF)

Table 1–2   The Frequency of Various Activities (Continued)

Frequency in Hertz	Application
88,000,000	FM radio
746,000,000	TV channel 60 (UHF)
824,000,000	Cellular phones
1,850,000,000	PCS phones
2,400,000,000	Wireless LAN
2,500,000,000	MMDS
4,200,000,000	Satellite big dish
9,000,000,000	Airborne radar
11,700,000,000	Satellite small dish
28,000,000,000	LMDS
500,000,000,000,000	Visible light
1,000,000,000,000,000,000	X-Files

Table 1–3 uses frequency to quantify some terms introduced earlier. These are not strict definitions, but rather general guidelines.

Table 1–3   Some Frequency Range Definitions

Term	Frequency Range
RF frequency	Less than 1 GHz
Microwave frequency	Between 1 GHz and 40 GHz
Millimeter wave frequency	Greater than 40 GHz

Apparently back in the old days, describing a signal's frequency based solely on a number was too simple, so early RF engineers decided to use letters to reference certain frequency ranges called *bands*. To make matters worse, just when everyone memorized these bands, they went ahead and changed them all. Just by way of entertainment, I have included some of the more popular (old) band designations in Table 1–4. Now when somebody describes a satellite as working in "C-Band," you will at least have an idea what range the signal's frequency is in.

You now know that a signal at 3 GHz can be referred to as either a 3 GHz signal, a microwave signal, or an S-Band signal.

Table 1–4 *Some Frequency Band Definitions*

Band	Frequency Range
L-Band	1.0-2.0 GHz
S-Band	2.0-4.0 GHz
C-Band	4.0-8.0 GHz
X-Band	8.0-12.0 GHz
Ku-Band	12.0-18.0 GHz

Did You Know?

Somewhere around 1889 a German physicist named Heinrich Hertz actually succeeded in generating the first airborne RF waves in his laboratory. For all his daring and brilliance, the RF engineers of the world have honored him by using his name as the unit of measure for frequency. I guess we're lucky the first RF wave wasn't generated by Heinrich Schmellingstonberger.

Digital Signals

The other type of electrical signal is a digital signal, which is the same type used in a computer. Unlike the (analog) sine wave signal, which varies gradually between its high points and low points, a digital signal is one which varies instantaneously between two electrical values. For all practical purposes, there are no values between the high and low levels in a digital signal. A digital signal is shown in Figure 1–3. Notice there are only two signal levels: up and down (high and low). Digital signals can represent information in the pattern of highs and lows. For instance, a certain pattern of highs and lows can be used to represent your voice as you talk on a cellular phone.

While digital signals are used to "represent" information, they aren't used to "carry" information over the air. Only analog signals (sine waves) are used to carry information "on their backs" as they travel through the air. These analog "carrier" signals can carry either analog or digital "information" signals. The process of combining information signals on top of carrier signals is called *modulation*, to be discussed later. When an information signal is combined with a carrier signal the result is known as wireless communications, and the analog signal doing the carrying is called RF or the *carrier* (go figure). An example of analog wireless communications is cellular telephony, the first generation of cellular phones. An example of digital wireless communications is Personal Communication Services (PCS), the second generation of cellular telephony. Both generations use RF to carry different formats of information.

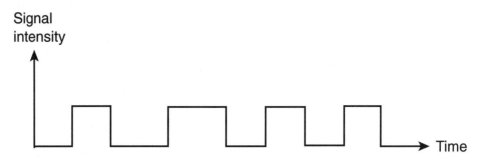

Figure 1–3   *A digital signal.*

Did You Know?

When a transmitter is always on and the RF signal comes out uninterrupted or continuously, that RF signal is referred to as a continuous wave (CW) RF signal. As you will learn later, there are actually wireless applications in which the transmitter is turned off and on rapidly, and the RF wave is not continuous. You might think that this type of RF signal would be referred to as a "discontinuous" wave RF signal, but it isn't. Just to keep things interesting, RF engineers refer to that type of RF signal as a pulsed RF signal.

You may be wondering which is better—analog or digital wireless communications? The simple answer is it depends, as both approaches have their pluses and minuses. Two things are certain, though. First, digital wireless communications is newer than analog so most wireless communication today (circa 1999) is still analog, and second, digital wireless communication interacts seamlessly with all other digital appliances, like computers. For this reason alone, I think it is safe to say that most, if not all, new wireless communications systems coming on line in the future will be digital.

2

RF Behavior

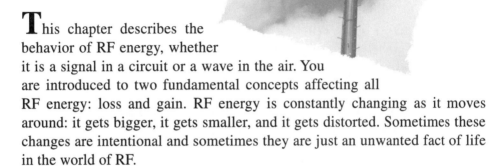

$\mathbf{T}$his chapter describes the
behavior of RF energy, whether
it is a signal in a circuit or a wave in the air. You
are introduced to two fundamental concepts affecting all
RF energy: loss and gain. RF energy is constantly changing as it moves
around: it gets bigger, it gets smaller, and it gets distorted. Sometimes these
changes are intentional and sometimes they are just an unwanted fact of life
in the world of RF.

You will learn how the concept of frequency can be expanded to describe a very important parameter of all RF items called *bandwidth*. The performance of any RF item depends on its bandwidth. Bandwidth can also be used to define an RF application's "boundary." All wireless applications are restricted to their predetermined frequency boundaries. In the United States, these boundaries are determined by the Federal Communications Commission (FCC), which has the authority to not only select the exact frequencies and uses for each bandwidth, but also has the responsibility to enforce their declarations. It ensures that no party transmits an RF signal at an unauthorized power level or frequency, or for an unauthorized use.

In this chapter, the concepts of absorption and reflection are used to describe what happens to RF waves as they encounter solid objects, which they often do when traveling around as waves. Some applications are adversely affected by this behavior, while others depend on it.

Finally, this chapter introduces you to an interesting term called *match* and its two methods of measurement: VSWR and return loss.

LOSS AND GAIN...

Devices

While an electrical signal is in the form of a current inside a transmitter or receiver, cruising around on some conductor, it encounters many different objects called *components* or *devices*. There are literally hundreds of different components which exist for some reason or another, but all components fall into one of two categories: active or passive. The difference is very simple. If it requires a power supply for it to work properly, it is an active component, otherwise, it is passive.

All components (active and passive) exhibit one of two properties: loss or gain. If the signal coming out is bigger than the signal going in, the device exhibits *gain*. If the device exhibits gain, it is called an *amplifier*. All amplifiers are active devices (i.e., they require a power supply). If you don't believe me, take the battery out of a cellular phone and try to make a call. In a cellular phone, the battery is connected to several amplifiers (among other things).

Attenuation

If the signal coming out is smaller than the signal going in, then the device exhibits *loss*. Any signal which passes through a device exhibiting loss is said to experience *attenuation* or is attenuated.

There are many different devices which exhibit loss; some are active and some are passive. You may be wondering (or maybe not), if a big RF signal goes in and a little RF signal comes out, what happens to the rest of the signal, the part that does not come out? It gets converted to heat. Components that exhibit loss warm up, components that exhibit a lot of loss get hot, and components that exhibit too much loss melt, which is why the power handling capability of passive devices is very important.

Figure 2–1 is a visual summary of gain and loss. The signal on the left experiences gain as it goes through the active device, as can be seen by the signal (represented by the sine wave) getting bigger. If the signal gets bigger, what must the device be? Here's a hint, it starts with "a" and ends with "mplifier." The signal on the right experiences loss, as the output signal is smaller than the input signal. If the signal gets smaller, what must the device be? This is a trick question, as it can be any one of a myriad of things, which will be discussed shortly.

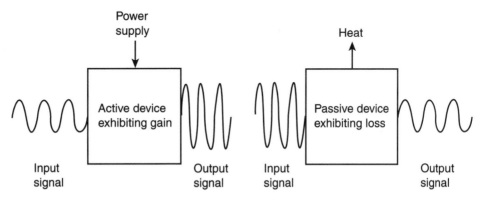

Figure 2–1   *Devices exhibiting gain and loss.*

If a signal coming out of an amplifier is ten times bigger than the signal going in, the amplifier has a gain of ten. If there are two of these amplifiers in a row, the resulting gain of both amplifiers is 100 (*not* 20!). If a signal is made ten times bigger and then that signal is made ten times bigger still, the final signal is 100 times bigger than the signal going into the first amplifier. It is simple multiplication (see Figure 2–2).

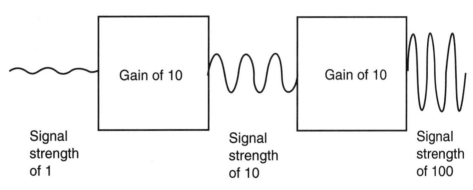

Figure 2–2   *The result of multiple gain stages.*

Insertion Loss

Passive devices exhibit the exact opposite behavior of active devices. If the signal coming out of a passive device is $1/100^{th}$ as big as the signal going in, then that device has a loss of 100 and the input signal is divided by 100 to find the magnitude of the output signal. If a signal has a strength of 100 watts and experiences a loss of 100, the output signal will be one watt. The loss a signal experiences as it goes through a passive component is referred to by RF engineers as *insertion loss* (IL). (Apparently, the word loss by itself just isn't descriptive enough.)

> ### Did You Know?
>
> Because of their heat dissipating property, most passive RF components are now rated with something called thermal impedance. The thermal impedance of a device is simply a measure of how hot it gets, given a certain amount of input power. The unit of measure for thermal impedance is degrees Celsius per watt.

DECIBELS ....

Definition

If mathematicians had never come along, the story might stop right here and you would be an expert on loss and gain. Unfortunately, however, the signals leaving a transmitter can be literally a *billion* times larger than the signals arriving at the receiver, and the multiplication and division of such disparate numbers can be quite unruly. So mathematicians came up with a way of representing these big numbers with smaller numbers, which allows the use of addition and subtraction in place of multiplication and division. They call this little trick *logarithms*. (Or, as some people affectionately refer to them, those nasty little things which nobody understood in Algebra.) Before you panic and throw out the book, logarithms (or logs) are really very simple. Trust me.

There are only two things you need to know about logs when used in the context of RF. First, logs are *always* a ratio of two values, and second, this ratio has units of decibels (named after some guy with the last name

Bel—really). Decibels are also referred to in the industry as dB (pronounced d´ b). For those of you who are gluttons for punishment, I have included the definition of dB here. Feel free to ignore it.

10log(Power out/Power in) measured in dB

Decibel Math

As mentioned above, if the signal coming out of an amplifier is 100 times bigger than the signal going in, then the amplifier has a gain of 100, or using the definition above, the same amplifier has a gain of 20 dB. Before you start scurrying to find your high school calculator, let me make matters really simple. There are only two dB conversions you are ever going to need. Take my word for it.

+3 dB means 2 times bigger (multiply by 2)
+10 dB means 10 times bigger (multiply by 10)

There are also two corollaries (remember Geometry?) you will need to know. First, if the number gets smaller, the dBs are negative.

−3 dB means 2 times smaller (divide by two)
−10 dB means 10 times smaller (divide by ten)

Second, dBs are only added or subtracted, they are never multiplied or divided. There, you're done. That is everything you need to know about logarithms and decibels. Now for a single illustrative example, see Example 2–1.

Now that you know how to do this conversion, you can forget it, as you will never need it again. The world of RF only deals in dB, so all you will ever have to do is add or subtract dBs at any point in the system to figure out what is going on.

Note: When a device exhibits loss, it is said to have a "loss of 6 dB." You must understand that this is equivalent to a change of -6 dB. It will not be referred to as a "loss of minus 6 dB."

Suppose there is the situation shown in Figure 2–3.

Example 2–1   *A simple decibel conversion.*

If a signal experiences a gain of 4000 (gets 4000 times bigger), what is the gain in dB?

It is best to break up the gain of 4000 into its simplest factors as shown below.

$$4000 = 10 \times 10 \times 10 \times 2 \times 2$$

Now you simply replace the multiplication of factors by the addition of dB (from the only two that you know).

$$4000 = 10 \text{ dB} + 10 \text{ dB} + 10 \text{ dB} + 3 \text{ dB} + 3 \text{ dB} = 36 \text{ dB}$$

A gain of 4000 is equivalent to a gain of 36 dB. What if it were a loss of 4000 instead of a gain? Simple. A loss of 4000 is equivalent to -36 dB. What if it were a gain of 5000, how would you utilize the only two conversions you know? Be creative.

$$5000 = 10 \times 10 \times 10 \times 10 \div 2$$

$$5000 = 10 \text{ dB} + 10 \text{ dB} + 10 \text{ dB} + 10 \text{ dB} - 3 \text{ dB} = 37 \text{ dB}$$

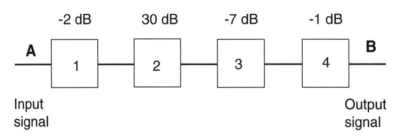

Figure 2–3   *Totaling up the decibels.*

An electrical signal at point A goes into component 1 with a loss of 2 dB, then goes to component 2 with a gain of 30 dB, then on to components 3 and 4 with losses of 7 dB and 1 dB, respectively. How big is the signal at point B with respect to the signal at point A? Has it experienced loss or gain? Since you are new at this, I will walk you through it, but in the future you are on your own.

The signal at point A minus 2 dB plus 30 dB minus 7 dB minus 1 dB equals the signal at point B. Therefore, the signal at point A plus 20 dB equals the signal at point B. Since 20 dB is being added to the signal at point A, the signal at point A gets bigger as it goes to point B, and therefore it experiences gain. In fact, it experiences exactly 20 dB of gain. Therefore, the signal at point B is 20 dB (or 100 times) bigger than at point A. If you understand this explanation, congratulate yourself, you have grasped a key element of RF.

But just to be sure, try one yourself. Referring to Figure 2–4, what is the size of the signal at point B with respect to the signal at point A?

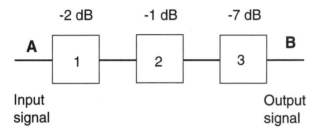

Figure 2–4 A decibel test.

The answer is −10 dB (1/10th the size). An interesting thing to note is that the lines connecting the devices in Figures 2–3 and 2–4 also exhibit insertion loss. Most of the time the loss in these "lines" is small and insignificant compared to the loss in the actual components, so it is ignored, but you should be aware of it. When a signal at one point in the system is 10 dB smaller than a signal at another point in the system, the smaller signal is said to be "10 dB down" from the larger signal.

Did You Know?

Probably the most famous expression in all of RF is the term "3 dB down." When a signal is referred to as being "3 dB down" from some reference signal, it means it's half as big. Sometimes RF engineers use the expression jokingly like, "I need to get my weight 3 dB down." Funny, huh?

BANDWIDTH ....

Definition

Probably no word is used more often in the world of RF than the word *bandwidth*. Now that you know what frequency is, it's not too difficult to understand the term bandwidth. Bandwidth is a way of describing a range of frequencies. It equals the difference between the highest frequency and the lowest frequency of the device or application, and therefore two frequencies are required to define a bandwidth. For instance, if a particular device can accommodate all frequencies between 75 MHz and 125 MHz, it has a bandwidth of 50 MHz (125 MHz–75 MHz).

Sometimes bandwidth is expressed in terms of a percentage. In this case, the bandwidth is simply divided by the average of the upper and lower frequencies. A simple example will explain everything (see Example 2–2).

Example 2–2 Calculating percentage bandwidth.

If a device can accommodate all frequencies between 75 MHz and 125 MHz, what is its percentage bandwidth?

First, you calculate the actual bandwidth. As noted above, the bandwidth for this example is 50 MHz (125 MHz–75 MHz).

Next, you calculate the average of the two frequencies. In this case it is 100 MHz (125 MHz + 75 MHz) ÷ 2.

Finally, you divide the bandwidth by the average frequency and multiply by 100%.

$$50 \text{ MHz} \div 100 \text{ MHz} \times 100\% = 50\%$$

A device which operates from 75 MHz to 125 MHz has a 50% bandwidth.

Octaves and Decades

There are two other important descriptors of bandwidth: *octave* and *decade*. Octave and decade come from the world of logarithms in which octave means twice as big and decade means ten times as big. If the upper frequency of a device is twice as big as the lower frequency, then the device has an octave bandwidth. For instance, a device which operates from 100 MHz to 200 MHz has an octave bandwidth. The same is true for a device whose lower frequency is 1.2 GHz and upper frequency is 2.4 GHz. To really confuse you, if the lower frequency of a device is 100 MHz and the upper frequency is 400 MHz, the device has a *two* octave bandwidth. Any device which has a bandwidth greater than one octave is said to have a multioctave bandwidth (as if it could be anything else).

If the upper frequency of a device is ten times the lower frequency, then the device has a decade bandwidth. An example of a decade bandwidth is a device which operates from 100 MHz to 1000 MHz (1 GHz).

WIDEBAND AND NARROWBAND...................................

Why is all this important? It is important because all RF components are classified as either *narrowband* (meaning narrow bandwidth) or *wideband* (meaning wide bandwidth). There are no hard and fast rules for the separation between narrowband and wideband, so I will make one up. If the bandwidth of a component is less than 50%, it is narrowband. If it is greater than 50%, it is wideband.

Ok, so where is all this leading? Here is the key: The wider the bandwidth of a component, the more frequencies it can accommodate, but the more it costs and the worse it performs. For instance, a narrowband passive component might have 1 dB of insertion loss (good), where an identical wideband passive component might have 3 or 4 dB of insertion loss (bad). The trick in designing an RF circuit is to get away with the narrowest bandwidth device possible while still accommodating all the frequencies required. As an example, cellular phone conversations—from the phone to the basestation—cover the frequency range 824–849 MHz. The most intelligent designs cover just this frequency range and no more.

An interesting thing to note (if you are really bored) is that narrowband and wideband devices are manufactured entirely different, which is why in the RF industry there are companies who specialize in either narrowband or wideband products.

RF IN THE ENVIRONMENT ....

Signal Behavior

Skin Effect

As you have already learned, RF signals are either on a conductor or flying around as waves in the air. When an RF signal is on a conductor, which is just about any piece of metal, it only hangs out on the surface of the metal object itself. Picture a solid piece of metal the shape of a brick. If an RF signal were placed on the brick, the signal itself would only be present on the surface of the brick, none would venture inside. If a detector could somehow be placed inside the brick, it would not detect the presence of the RF signal. This behavior exhibited by RF signals is called the *skin effect*, which is self-explanatory.

The reason the skin effect occurs is simple to understand, if you have a degree in electrical engineering. But since the assumption is that you don't have an engineering degree—or you are an engineer with too much free time—I will explain the skin effect as follows. RF signals have a natural inclination to want to escape solid objects and fly around in the air, but for reasons which will be explained later, they cannot always do it. The next best thing these restless RF signals can do is to get as close to the outside of whatever it is they are on in the hope of ultimately escaping and fulfilling their true destiny: to be detected by aliens from another galaxy.

Absorption

Once an RF signal does escape the bounds of a conductor and flies around in the air, just about everything it encounters changes it in some way. These changes tend to do one of two things to the RF signal: they either make it smaller or change the direction in which it is traveling.

Most of the "things" the RF signal encounters tend to make the signal smaller, including the air we breathe, rain, glass, wood, and even foliage. In a very real sense, all of these "things" can be viewed as types of passive devices with some amount of insertion loss (expressed in dB, of course). This insertion loss exhibited by things in nature is called *absorption*, because it absorbs the RF signal.

A perfect example to demonstrate absorption is the effect rain has on direct-to-home satellite TV, which is predominantly in the Ku-Band. It just so happens that the size of the RF signal carrying direct-to-home satellite television is just about the size of an average raindrop, which makes the conditions ideal for absorption. When the weather is clear, the signal makes it to the receiver with only nominal loss and everything is fine. But when it starts to rain, some of the signal gets absorbed by the rain and, therefore, less of it finds its way to the little satellite dish on the roof. During instances of very heavy rain, it is entirely possible that absorption will be severe enough to wipe out the signal, leaving the direct-to-home satellite TV service out of order. This situation is not something the service providers advertise, but it is something you should be aware of if you live in, say, Seattle.

At the risk of insulting you, when an RF signal experiences loss as it travels through a rainstorm, where does the lost energy go? HEAT! Believe it or not, the rain actually warms up. Of course the rise in temperature is so small it is difficult to measure, not to mention the darn raindrop would probably evaporate before you could get out the thermometer.

Even the air we breathe absorbs RF energy as it travels, which explains why RF signals cannot travel forever and why a cellular phone call drops out when the mobile unit strays too far from a basestation. Now for the $64,000 question. When does a cellular phone have the greater call range, on a sunny day or on a rainy day? I will leave the answer up to you.

Reflection

Not everything an RF wave encounters absorbs RF energy. Some things which RF waves encounter send the RF signal in another direction. This change of direction is called *reflection*. As an approximation, RF signals tend to reflect off objects at the same angle at which they encounter them (see Figure 2–5).

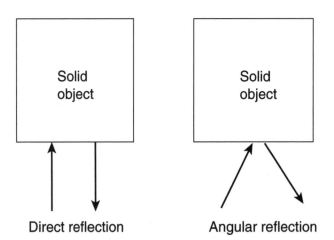

Direct reflection   Angular reflection

Figure 2–5   Direct and angular reflection.

Many objects reflect, at least partially, RF signals which hit them. The amount of reflection depends on two things: the frequency of the RF (of course), and the material of the object. Some materials reflect RF energy only moderately, like concrete, while others reflect it completely, like metal. For materials which only partially reflect the RF wave, what do you suppose happens to the rest of the signal? I'll give you a hint. Go back a few paragraphs to the one which contains the word absorption. Now you've got it. When an RF signal hits any material, the RF energy either gets completely absorbed (like water), partially absorbed and partially reflected (like concrete), or completely reflected (like metal). Congratulations, you now understand RF behavior.

MATCH ....

What is Match?

The Meaning of 50 Ohms

Before an RF signal becomes airborne, it spends its existence cruising around on a conductor or inside some component. Every component has an entrance or exit, or both. It is easiest to think of the conductor and the components as parts of a garden hose system with the RF signal as the water inside. If an RF signal is to traverse a conductor and then enter a component, the conductor (garden hose) needs to be connected to the component (a sprinkler). That seems simple enough.

Because engineers run the RF world, no two garden hoses are exactly the same size. So no matter what conductor is connected to what component, some of the RF signal (water) leaks out. (No surprise there.) To make their lives easier, engineers in the RF world have standardized the size of the hose they all agree to use. In this way, a conductor (or component) made by one company will more or less work with a component made by another company—with only a little leaking. If I were actually talking about hoses, the standard size might be specified as "one half inch diameter." Since I'm talking about RF, the standard (hose) size is specified as 50 ohms (named after some famous engineer). Ohms are a measure of *impedance*, which describes the difficulty the RF signal (water) has in passing through the conductor (hose). There is no real significance to the 50 ohms, other than everyone agrees to make their RF stuff (garden hoses) that size.

The first thing RF engineers want to know, now that they have agreed to this standard size, is how much their hoses will leak when connected to someone else's. This is important to know because the goal is to get a certain amount of RF signal from one conductor or component to another, and if too much of it leaks out, the system will not work right.

VSWR

To measure the amount of leaking, RF engineers coined a term called *VSWR* (pronounced viz´ wär). Technically, VSWR stands for Voltage Standing Wave Ratio, but you'll do yourself a favor if you pretend you never read that. VSWR is a numerical measurement of this thing called *match*. The better the match, the less the leaking.

The formula for VSWR is complicated, and to make matters worse, its unit of measure is nothing. It has no units. It does, however, have a format of X:1 (read "X to one"), where the bigger the X, the more it leaks (see Table 2–1).

Table 2–1   The Meaning of VSWR

VSWR	Meaning
1.0:1	Perfect match, a hose with no leaking, cannot be done.
1.4:1	Excellent match, very little leaking, often a design goal.
2.0:1	Good match, acceptable amount of leaking.
10:1	Horrible match, a result of designing a circuit after reading this book.
∞:1	As a result of trying to hook up a garden hose to the Lincoln Tunnel.[a]

a. For those of you fortunate enough to have avoided calculus, ∞ means infinity.

Return Loss

Because RF engineers refuse to leave well enough alone, one measure of match is not enough. There is another measure of match called *return loss*, which is measured in, of all things, dB. There is a very straightforward formula for converting from VSWR to dB, but since no one can remember it (including most RF engineers), a conversion chart similar to the one shown in Table 2–2 is used. As you can see, the larger the VSWR, the smaller the return loss.

Table 2-2 *VSWR versus Return Loss*

VSWR	Return Loss (dB)
1.0:1	∞
1.4:1	15.6
2.0:1	9.5
10:1	1.7
∞:1	0

Consequences of an Imperfect Match

As much as I enjoy condemning RF engineers for unnecessarily complicating matters, there is a good reason for using the term return loss. When the match is not perfect and the hose leaks, the water (RF) does not actually leak out. In reality, the RF energy heads back down in the direction from which it came. When RF energy starts heading back down in the direction from which it came, it is called *reflection* (sound familiar?). Since no match is perfect, there is always some RF energy which is reflected. Frequently, the amount of RF energy reflected is small, in which case it goes unnoticed. In situations where the match is poor and a lot of RF energy gets reflected, the device it came from tends to blow up, which is generally how a bad match is discovered.

Did You Know?

There are actually two extreme cases for return loss: a perfect open and a perfect short. A perfect open occurs when someone forgets to connect the rest of the circuit to the output of a component and the RF signal encounters nothing but air. A perfect short occurs when someone lays a screwdriver across a perfect open. In both cases, almost all of the RF energy is reflected and the VSWR approaches ∞. Needless to say, this situation should generally be avoided, unless blowing up RF components seems like fun.

Impedance matching

Quite often in the world of RF circuit design an engineer is forced to connect two things (a conductor to a component) with a bad match. For instance, the conductor may have the correct "size" (impedance) of 50 ohms, but the device it is attached to has a size (impedance) of 100 ohms. Connecting these two items as is would result in a bad match, and the circuit would not work very well, as there would be a great deal of power reflected. What do RF engineers do in this situation—after they get done crying? They insert, between the two disparate impedances, a neat little bit of technology called an *impedance matching* circuit. In the example above, the impedance matching circuit changes the 100 ohm impedance to 50 ohms, so the two items can be properly connected. Figure 2–6 is a graphical representation of an impedance matching circuit.

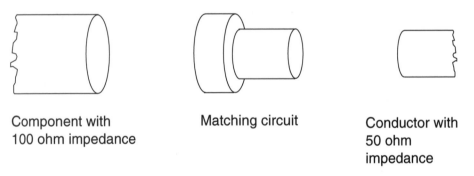

Component with   Matching circuit   Conductor with
100 ohm impedance   50 ohm
                                                            impedance

Figure 2–6   *A graphical representation of a matching circuit.*

As will be discussed later, impedance matching circuits come in many different varieties, but they all serve the same purpose: to change some RF item's impedance to 50 ohms.

Part 2

RF Hardware

3

Basic System
Components

This chapter begins by presenting block diagrams
of the components that comprise the two basic building blocks in all wireless systems: transmitters and receivers. Once you understand how transmitters and receivers work, and the roles they play, you are well on your way to understanding wireless communications. And the good news is, both of these building blocks are fairly simple to look at and to understand because they consist of just *five* different RF components, which are covered in this chapter.

This chapter explains what roles antennas, amplifiers, filters, and mixers play in changing the nature, size, shape, and frequency of RF signals. It also points out where RF signals come from in the first place: sources. Each section within this chapter demonstrates that these five fundamental components all come in different variations, to accomplish very specific objectives. This usually involves manufacturing the device in such a way as to optimize one or two key performance parameters, which naturally increases its price. Appendix B is a comprehensive list of the many parameters used to quantify RF component performance.

Manufacturers in the RF industry are always trying to improve these five components by making them smaller, lighter, more energy efficient, and at lower cost. High volume wireless products, like cellular phones, have increased the demand for these items, which has served to drive down their cost dramatically. State of the art is constantly changing for these items, as competition spurs innovation. For instance, there are at least 30 companies that manufacture high power amplifiers for wireless infrastructure, which will ultimately translate to lower prices and more features for you, the consumer.

Finally, this chapter concludes with a review of the two basic building blocks just to make sure you were paying attention.

BLOCK DIAGRAMS ....

Transmitters and receivers are very complex systems with many internal components, but all transmitters and receivers perform the same basic functions and they can both be described by simple block diagrams (see Figures 3–1 and 3–2). In these figures, the signals flow from left to right. The weird shaped things are the components and the straight lines are the conductors which connect them. As can be seen in these block diagrams, a signal gets from one component to another by way of a conductor. Recall that a receiver turns an airborne wave into an electrical signal and a transmitter turns an electrical signal into an airborne wave.

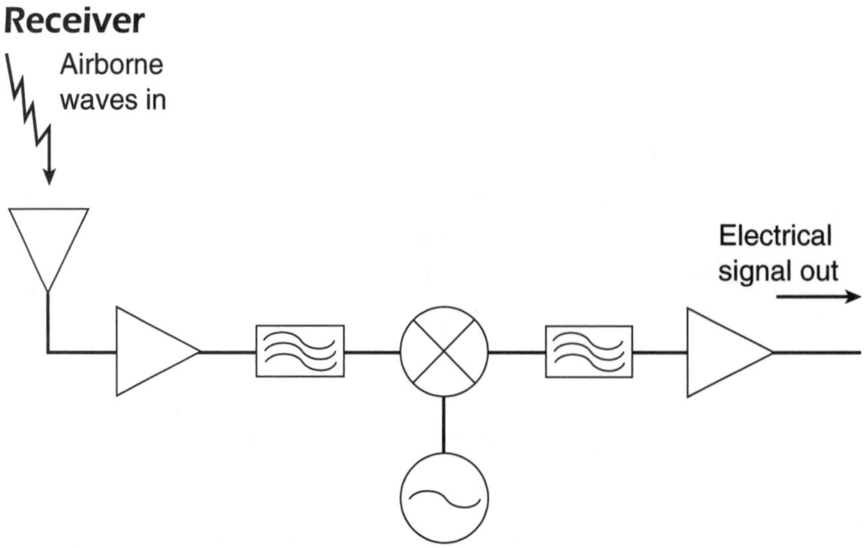

Receiver

Figure 3–1   Receiver block diagram.

Transmitter

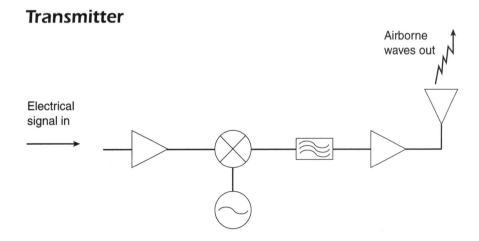

Figure 3–2   *Transmitter block diagram.*

At their simplest, all transmitters and receivers consist of just five basic building blocks. (Notice in Figures 3–1 and 3–2 there are only five distinct items in each block diagram, although some of them are repeated.) Once you understand these five building blocks and what functions they perform, you are half way to understanding RF systems and wireless communications. (You will learn about the other half in the section on Modulation.) I will discuss each of these building blocks and what roles they perform in a wireless system.

ANTENNAS ....

Block Diagram

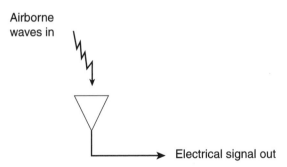

Figure 3–3   *Block diagram of an antenna.*

This first device is called an *antenna* (see Figure 3–3). If you only learn one thing from this book, learn this: *Every wireless system has an antenna.* You may not see it, you may not recognize it, but it is there. The antenna's job is very simple—it converts electrical signals flowing down a conductor into airborne waves (in a transmitter) *or* it converts airborne waves into electrical signals flowing down a conductor (in a receiver) *or* both. It is the heart of the wireless system: no antenna, no wireless communications. Visually, it can be viewed as airborne waves entering (or leaving) the funnel-like structure at the top in the block diagram and leaving (or entering) as current along the conductor at the bottom of the block diagram. When airborne waves leave an antenna they are said to *radiate* out from the antenna. Most antennas work equally well in both directions.

Antenna Characteristics

Active and Passive

Antennas can be active devices or passive devices. Passive antennas are just a hunk of metal, configured in a very specific way. If the antenna is active, it has a power supply attached somewhere. Active antennas are nothing more than passive antennas with amplifiers inside of them. You will learn more about amplifiers in the next chapter.

> **Did You Know?**
>
> Most active antennas have only one electrical connection. It carries both the RF signal *and* the power signal on the same conductor, which cuts down on material costs, not to mention the extra five seconds it would take to make another connection. Every little bit helps.

Sizes and Shapes

As you have probably already observed, antennas come in many shapes and sizes, from the super large towers transmitting AM radio signals, to the small and large dishes receiving satellite signals, to the little rubber ducky antennas on cellular phones. A variety of antennas is shown in Figure 3–4. Figure 3–5 shows a cellular basestation tower where the vertical structures at the top are the antennas.

The shape and size of any particular antenna depends on only two things. The first thing an antenna design depends on is the frequency which it is designed to handle. As a general rule, the lower the frequency the antenna must handle, the larger the antenna, which is why AM radio stations, broadcasting at 530 kHz (530,000 Hertz), have antennas several hundred feet high while cellular phones, operating at 900 MHz (900,000,000 Hertz), have antennas only six inches long.

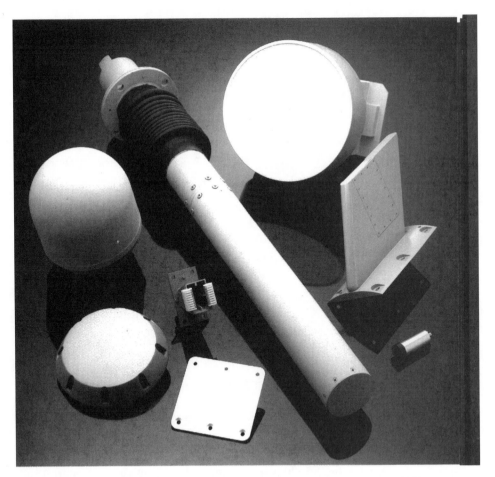

Figure 3–4   *A sampling of antennas. Courtesy of M/A-Com, an AMP company.*

The second thing which determines the size and shape of an antenna is the direction of the airborne signal. If the objective is to transmit or receive

Figure 3–5   *Basestation antennas.*
Courtesy of Alpha Industries

the airborne signal in all directions equally, then the antenna will have a certain shape. Antennas of this type are referred to as *omni-directional* antennas, meaning "all directions." If, on the other hand, the objective is to transmit (or receive) the airborne signal in only one direction (north for instance), then the antenna will have a completely different shape. Antennas of this type are simply referred to as—don't laugh—directional antennas.

Signal Strength and Direction

Why do RF systems engineers choose one antenna type over another, besides the fact that they're bored? In the case of a transmitted signal, since there is only a finite amount of RF energy going into the antenna as current, unless you believe in the tooth fairy, there can only be a finite amount of energy coming out of the antenna as airborne waves. If an omnidirectional antenna is used, all of the RF energy must be evenly divided in all directions. If the antenna is in the middle of a big city or part of a cellular phone, then an omnidirectional antenna is fine. But what if the antenna is up against a mountain? Radiating some of the RF energy directly into the mountain is a waste—unless there are mole people living inside the mountain trying to pick up HBO. A directional antenna, radiating RF energy strictly away from the mountain, will actually radiate more RF energy away from the mountain than an omnidirectional antenna. Both antennas will have the same amount of RF energy coming out, but since the directional antenna has to divide its energy over a smaller area, that area receives more RF energy. Here is an analogy to help you visualize this phenomenon. Suppose you were to bake two apple pies and the first pie is a normal one, with the ingredients covering the whole pie tin. This is analogous to the omni-directional antenna as all the calories (RF energy) are spread evenly over the whole pie tin. The second pie has the same exact amount of ingredients as the first pie, but in this case the ingredients are somehow constrained to half the pie tin. This is analogous to the directional antenna. Each slice of the "half" pie will contain more calories (RF energy) than an equivalent size slice of the normal pie.

As you probably know from personal experience, the signal strength radiating out of an antenna decreases in strength the farther away you get from the antenna. (You should recall from a previous chapter that this behavior is a result of absorption.) That is why radio station reception fades as you get farther outside a city's limits. Therefore, a directional antenna with its higher power over a smaller area will have a greater signal range than an omnidirectional antenna with the same output power, which means you can listen to your favorite oldies station that much longer.

How Antennas Work

Wavelength

How the antenna actually does what it does requires a rigorous understanding of mathematics, physics, and electronics and is way beyond the scope of this book, but that won't keep me from trying to explain it. Assume for the sake of discussion that there is this thing call a *wavelength* which measures the length of an RF signal. Further assume that this wavelength is inversely proportional to the signal's frequency, which means the higher the frequency, the shorter the wavelength. To illustrate the point, a cellular phone's RF signal (900 MHz) is higher in frequency than an AM radio's signal (530 kHz), and therefore the cellular phone's signal has a shorter wavelength. Antennas begin to radiate RF energy (as waves) when the length of the wavelength of the RF signal it is carrying becomes similar in length to that of the antenna itself. The electrical current flowing into the antenna begins to radiate out of the antenna as invisible waves. Basically, it is magic. And of course the opposite is also true. Invisible waves, of appropriate wavelength, going into the antenna come out as current flowing down a conductor. All this explains why a cellular phone, which receives signals with a one foot wavelength, needs only a six-inch antenna. A six-foot antenna would not work very well and neither would a half-inch antenna.

Antennas explain how the RF energy "escapes" from solid objects as briefly mentioned during the discussion of skin effect. Of course in this case the solid object is an antenna. In reality, any metallic object which is about as big as the wavelength of the RF signal on it, will act as an antenna, and the RF energy will begin to radiate out from it. As hinted at before, if the object is much smaller than the wavelength it will not radiate RF energy at all, and if the object is much bigger than the wavelength, the object will radiate some RF energy, but not very efficiently.

Antenna Performance

Antenna Patterns

Because antenna design is still mostly an art requiring trial and error, RF engineers need a tool to know if the antenna they have designed actually does what they want. The tool they utilize is called an *antenna pattern*. In its simplest form, an antenna pattern is nothing more than a birds-eye view of the RF energy radiating out from an antenna. In an antenna pattern, a solid dot in the middle represents the antenna and a line drawn around the antenna represents the power radiating out from the antenna. By convention, the line is drawn where the power radiating out from the antenna drops to one half that of the power at the antenna itself. Two representative antenna patterns are shown in Figure 3–6.

Did You Know?

What is true for antennas is also true for the RF world in general: the higher the frequency, the smaller things become. One of the reasons today's cellular phones are so small is that they operate at frequencies high enough to allow the components inside to be made small enough to fit inside the phone. Here are the wavelengths of three common wireless applications:

AM radio:	566 meters (3 city blocks)
Cellular telephony:	1 foot
Direct-to-home satellite TV:	1 inch

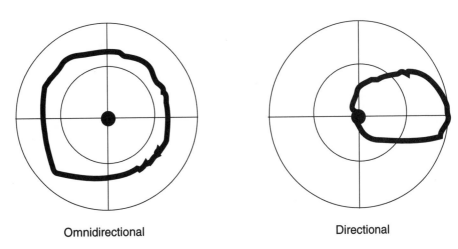

| Omnidirectional | Directional |

Figure 3–6   Antenna patterns.

As you can see on the left side of Figure 3–6, there is a (more or less) circular pattern drawn equidistant from the center, which is the antenna. This is a typical omnidirectional antenna pattern and shows RF energy radiated equally in all directions. On the right side of Figure 3–4 is one of many possible directional antenna patterns. Notice that all the RF energy is radiated to the right of the antenna, which is still in the center. This antenna pattern might be used for radiating RF energy down a narrow mountain pass between two tall mountains. Forget the mole people.

Did You Know?

There is actually a new family of antennas called intelligent antennas. Believe it or not, these antennas can actually change their antenna patterns instantaneously to facilitate communicating with individual users. It's like having a basestation antenna assigned just to you. Now wouldn't that make you feel special?

Polarization

When RF waves travel in the air, the sine waves themselves have an orientation to them: either vertical or horizontal. This orientation is called *polarization*, which is very easy to visualize. If a cellular phone is held in such a way that the antenna is straight up and down, the RF (sine) wave coming out will be vertically polarized (the sine wave will vary up and down as it travels). However, if a cellular phone is held in such a way that the antenna is sideways, then the signal coming out will be horizontally polarized and the sine wave will vary from side to side as it travels.

Did You Know?

If you have ever watched a 3-D movie wearing those funny cardboard glasses, you've experienced the effects of polarization firsthand. All electromagnetic waves, not just RF, are comprised of traveling sine waves. Visible light is made up of horizontal and vertical sine waves. In 3-D movies, two slightly different images, with different polarization, are projected. Each side of the glasses lets only one type of polarization pass, which causes each eye to see a different image, tricking you into thinking you see an image with depth.

What is the purpose of all this? Polarization is a way to fit two different signals, of the identical frequency, in the same place at the same time. If the cellular signal you are trying to receive is vertically (up and down) polarized, as most cellular signals are, and you hold a cellular phone with the antenna horizontal, you will pick up a weak signal. As you turn the cellular phone's antenna upward, the signal strength will increase until it is fully upright.

The goal of all RF systems is to fit as much information (phone conversations) into the limited bandwidth it is allotted, and polarization does just that, by allowing two otherwise identical signals to be differentiated solely by their different polarizations. In theory, by using horizontal and vertical polarization, twice as many conversations can take place in the same bandwidth.

Because RF engineers have too much free time on their hands, they figured out that if a vertically polarized signal is combined with a horizontally polarized signal, what results is a whole new type of polarization called *circular polarization*. In this form of polarization, the RF sine wave continuously varies from horizontal to vertical as it travels.

> **Did You Know?**
>
> There are actually two different kinds of circular polarization. (I told you they have too much free time.) One type is called Right Hand Circular or RHC and the other, naturally, is called Left Hand Circular or LHC.

Antenna Dimensions

One-Dimensional Antennas

As mentioned before, there are many different shapes of antennas, but they tend to fall into one of two categories: one-dimensional antennas and two-dimensional antennas. One-dimensional antennas are made from a hunk of wire in either a straight line, like those used on a cellular phone, or some clever shape, like the old rabbit ear antennas found on televisions before the advent of cable.

Two-Dimensional Antennas

Two-dimensional antennas offer a lot more variety, from patches and arrays to horns and dishes. A patch antenna is essentially a square hunk of metal, while an array is a bunch of patches in an organized, two-dimensional pattern. Examples of both can be seen in Figures 3–7a and 3–7b. Horn antennas resemble the megaphones used by old-time high school cheerleaders.

Figure 3–7a Patch antennas. *Courtesy of Alpha Industries.*

Figure 3–7b An array antenna. *Courtesy of Epsilon Lambda Electronics, Inc.*

Dish antennas act as big funnels collecting the RF energy which comes their way, mostly from satellites. Dishes come in many sizes—from the ul-tra-huge ones employed by the local television stations to the little 18-inch ones used for direct-to-home satellite TV. The size of the dish depends on two things, the first of which you should know by now: frequency. The high-er the frequency, the smaller the dish required. The second thing which im-pacts the size of the dish is the power transmitted by the other party. The greater the transmitted power, the smaller the dish needs to be. As you can now appreciate, direct-to-home satellite TV, with its small dish, was only made possible by the latest generation of satellites capable of transmitting at higher frequency and higher power. A large dish antenna is shown in Figure 6–9 (in the forthcoming section on Satellite Communications).

AMPLIFIERS...

Block Diagram

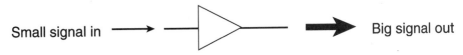

Figure 3–8   Block diagram of an amplifier.

This next device, shown in Figure 3–8, is called an amplifier, which makes signals bigger. RF signals constantly need to be made bigger as they move from place to place. It's just like driving a car. You drive around from place to place using up gas, and when you run low, you fill up. An amplifier is a filling station for RF signals. They move around from place to place (either in the air or along a conductor) and when they need a boost, hopefully there is an amplifier around. Visually, a small signal enters the large end of the block diagram (left side) and leaves as a large signal from the pointy end.

Fundamental Properties of Amplifiers

Gain

There are three fundamental properties of all amplifiers: gain, noise or power, and linearity. Gain is a measure of how much bigger the output signal is than the input signal, and is measured in, as you may have guessed, dB. Some places in an RF system need a lot of gain (40 or 50 dB), and some places only need a little (5-10 dB).

Amplifiers fall into three main categories: low noise, high power, and "other." A low noise amplifier is the very first amplifier a signal encounters after it comes through the antenna in a receiver. High power amplifiers are the last amplifier a signals goes through before it flies out the antenna in a transmitter. Every other amplifier is an "other."

Noise Figure

Low noise amplifiers (LNA) listen for very small RF signals so they must be vewy, vewy, qwiet. A measure of an LNA's quietness is called *noise figure* (NF) and is measured in, of course, dB. The fundamental property of an LNA is noise figure. The lower the NF of an LNA, the better. Some RF engineers pay big bucks for an LNA with super low NF. (The rest of us just invest in mutual funds.) What is a good NF? It depends. Think of it this way: the lower the noise figure, the smaller the signal which the LNA can hear, the further away the LNA can be, and thus the greater the range, of say, a cellular phone.

Output Power

High power amplifiers (HPA) boost the RF signal as big as possible (or allowable) just before it is shot out of the antenna. The bigger the signal, the farther it travels and the greater the range, of say, a cellular phone. The second fundamental property of an HPA is output power, measured in watts. Generally speaking, the higher the power, the better.

Unfortunately, RF engineers insist on making things difficult and tend to express output power in *dBm*. What the heck is dBm you ask? It literally means "dB above one milliwatt." For instance, 10 dBm is a signal 10 dB above (or bigger than) 1 mW, 30 dBm is 30 dB bigger than 1 mW, and so on. A 30 dBm signal, which is 30 dB (or 1000 times) bigger than 1 mW, translates to one watt (1000 x 1 mWatt). So 30 dBm is the same as 1 watt. Damn engineers. See Table 3–1 for some common conversions.

Table 3–1   Watts to dBm Conversion

Power in Watts	Power in dBm
0.1 mW	-10 dBm
1 mW	0 dBm
1 watt	30 dBm
1000 watts	60 dBm

Figure 3–9a shows an example of an LNA and Figure 3–9b shows an exaggerated example of an HPA. The two were chosen to demonstrate how much bigger HPAs can be compared to LNAs. This situation arises out of the need to remove heat from the HPA. Because amplifiers are not 100% efficient, some of the energy that goes into the amplifier comes out as an RF signal, but the remainder comes out as heat, which is why many HPAs contain fans to provide internal cooling, like the fan in a car's engine. If the HPA's fans stop working, you might as well get out the marshmallows.

When discussing the output power of an HPA you need to know that everything is relative. For instance, while the output amplifier in most cellular phones puts out less than 1 watt, the output amplifier at the basestation end puts out 50 watts and both amplifiers are referred to as HPAs. Just because it is referred to as an HPA does not mean it puts out a lot of power.

Figure 3–9a An LNA. *Courtesy of Mini-Circuits*

Figure 3–9b An HPA. *Courtesy of Amplifier Research*

Linearity

In this age of digital communications there is a third fundamental property of amplifiers called *linearity*. One of the implications of digital wireless communications is that when a digital signal rides on top of an RF carrier, any amplifier which the signal goes through must be really linear. Linearity is a measure of how much the amplifier distorts the shape of the signal. As you will learn in the future section on modulation, tiny changes to the shape of the RF carrier (sine wave) actually contain information; therefore, unwanted changes in the signal's shape serve only to distort the information. What RF engineers want at the output of their amplifiers is a signal which is bigger than, but identical in shape to, the input signal. As a way of visual introduction to the concept of linearity, I present you with the single most important piece of information about any amplifier, the *transfer curve* (see Figure 3–10). A transfer curve is a graph of the output power versus the input power of an amplifier. All amplifiers display this type of behavior.

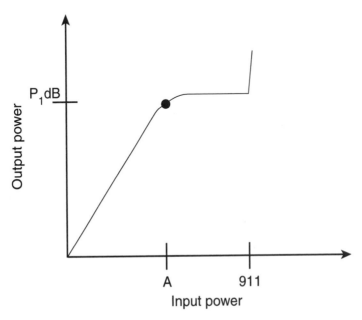

Figure 3–10 Output power versus input power of an amplifier.

Referring to Figure 3–10, as the input power to an amplifier increases (moving to the right on the horizontal axis), the output power from the amplifier increases by a like amount, at least until the point marked "A." Everything up to point A is known as the linear region of an amplifier. It is in this region which the amplifier must operate if it is to avoid distorting the RF signal. The output power at point A is referred to as the P_1dB (pronounced p wun´ d b) point or the P_1dB power or the one dB compression point. P_1dB has an exact definition, but it will only cause confusion. It is much simpler to think of the P_1dB point of an amplifier as the highest power the amplifier can put out *and* still be in the linear region. Or another way of viewing it, P_1dB is the highest linear power an amplifier can put out.

Beyond point A on the horizontal axis (increasing the input power further), notice that the output power no longer rises, but stays flat. In other words, an increase in input power no longer results in an increase in output power. The amplifier stops amplifying. After point A, the amplifier is said to be in *saturation* and enters the non-linear region. It is in the non-linear region where all the signal distortion occurs and messes up a cellular phone call. Output power greater than P_1dB is referred to as saturated output power. In some instances, saturated output power is useful, but not in digital wireless communications. Just as a note: if the input power is increased further, eventually a point is reached where the output power of the amplifier increases rapidly, as shown. Of course at this point the output power is in the form of flames shooting out of the amplifier, which is why it is referred to (jokingly) as the 911 point.

One method of measuring an amplifier's linearity is by its *intercept point* (which is often referred to as the *third order intercept point*). The higher the intercept point, the more linear the amplifier. The intercept point is represented by the symbol Ip3 (pronounced i´ pee three). (Sometimes an amplifier's Ip3 is referred to as its *dynamic range*.) Like power, the intercept point is also measured in dBm. An amplifier with a 40 dBm intercept point is more linear than an amplifier with a 30 dBm intercept point. A rule of thumb used by all RF engineers is that an amplifier's Ip3 is 10 dB greater than its P_1dB point. There is no need to go any further.

Did You Know?

The third order intercept point is actually a mythical point that does not really exist and cannot be measured directly. Instead, a bunch of other measurements are made and then the Ip3 of an amplifier is calculated using these other measurements. Leave it to RF engineers to base the performance of this critical component on something that doesn't even exist.

How Amplifiers Work

How an amplifier supplies gain to an input signal is an interesting process. The input signal itself does not actually get bigger per se as it moves through the amplifier. Instead, the input RF signal acts to control another type of power called DC power, where DC stands for direct current. (DC power or DC voltage, unlike a sine wave, does not vary with time, but is constant, just as the voltage from the battery in a flashlight.) Similar to turning the tires of an automobile, as you drive you aren't really turning the tires themselves, you are controlling the tires' movement with a controller called the steering wheel. If the automobile were an amplifier, the driver would be the input RF signal, the tires would be the DC power, and the steering wheel would be the controller called a *transistor*, which you will learn about in a later chapter. In an amplifier, the RF input signal tells the transistor to "shape" the DC power to exactly reflect the shape of the input signal. In this way, the output signal has the same exact shape as the input signal, only bigger. How much bigger? It depends on how much DC input power there is. The main difference between HPAs and every other amplifier is that HPAs have greater DC input power.

Special Amplifiers

Limiting Amplifiers

There are two special cases of amplifiers which you should be aware of if you really want to impress an RF engineer. The first type is called a *limiting amplifier* and, as the name implies, it limits the output power. This type of amplifier is used in places where the component which follows it will be damaged if its input power is too high. The limiting amplifier provides a sort of protection for the next component. You may recall from Figure 3–10 that all amplifiers behave somewhat as limiting amplifiers. At a certain input power, the output power levels off. Basically, the only difference between a limiting amplifier and any other amplifier is that limiting amplifiers do not blow up at the 911 point—in theory.

Balanced Amplifiers

The other type of amplifier is called a *balanced amplifier*. It is not so much a different amplifier as it is a different amplifier design. In a balanced amplifier, there are two amplifiers in parallel (see Figure 3–11).

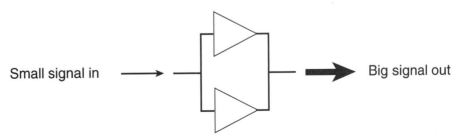

Small signal in ⟶   ⟹ Big signal out

Figure 3–11 Block diagram of a balanced amplifier.

Referring to Figure 3–11, in a balanced amplifier design the RF signal enters at the left side as usual. Once inside, the signal gets split in two, with half going to one amplifier and half going to the other amplifier. Once inside the amplifiers, both "half" signals get amplified and are then added together before leaving at the output on the right side. From the outside, a balanced amplifier looks and behaves just like a regular amplifier.

At this point you must be wondering why go through all that if one amplifier will do. Well, there are two advantages to the balanced amplifier design which just cannot be realized from a single amplifier. The first advantage is that there are two amplifiers. If one fails, there is still one working, albeit with reduced performance. Balanced amplifiers are often used in circumstances requiring a high degree of reliability or fault tolerance.

The second advantage—and you are going to have to take my word for it because it is too complicated to explain—is that balanced amplifiers provide a better match (lower VSWR) than regular amplifiers. They leak less, and less leaking is premium performance which some RF systems simply must have to function properly.

Did You Know?

Amplifier prices vary dramatically. In general, the higher the frequency or the wider the bandwidth or the greater the output power, the more the amplifier costs. Also, super low noise figure amplifiers are expensive. Just as an example, some low cost surface-mount amplifiers sell for as little as 50¢, while some high power, wideband amplifiers sell for as much as $50,000. Just be glad you don't have an RF engineer on your Christmas shopping list.

Variable Gain Amplifiers

There is one last amplifier type you should know about, the *variable gain amplifier* or VGA. Most amplifiers have fixed gain (i.e., the gain has one single value). A fixed gain amplifier with 10 dB of gain will make all input signals ten times bigger. Variable gain amplifiers have an external control which allows the user to vary the gain over some predefined range. All VGAs come specified with a "gain range" like 10–20 dB, for example. A VGA is like a gas range, where the heat (gain) varies from simmer to boil and the external control is the knob on the stove. The block diagram of a VGA is shown in Figure 3–12 and, as you can see, it is nothing more than a regular amplifier with an arrow through it.

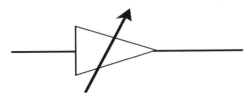

Figure 3–12 Block diagram of a variable gain amplifier.

In practice, rarely is a VGA's external control connected to the outside world, like the knob on a stove. More often than not, the VGA's control is connected to some other point in the RF system that senses what is going on and changes the VGA's gain accordingly. Whenever a component changes its own performance based on something happening somewhere else in the system, it is known as *feedback*. VGAs frequently sense an RF signal "farther down the line." If the signal it is sensing is too big, it lowers its own gain, and if the signal isn't big enough, it cranks it up. It continues changing its own gain until the signal it is sensing is just right, and then it keeps its gain right at that point.

Did You Know?

There is an entire branch of electronics called feedback theory, which predicts the behavior of feedback circuits. The thermostat controlling a home's temperature is a classic example of feedback theory. All feedback circuits work the same way, by sensing an output (room temperature) and varying an input (furnace flames) to achieve a specific outcome (desired temperature). RF systems, like all electrical systems, make extensive use of feedback circuits. I guess the components don't like it when it gets too cold.

FILTERS..

Block Diagram

Figure 3–13 Block diagram of a filter.

This next device in the lineup is called a *filter* (see Figure 3–13). The filter does just what you think it does—it filters out all the signals which are not wanted. Visually it can be viewed as a bunch of signals at different frequencies entering the filter on the left (f_1, f_2, and f_3) and only the desired signal (at the desired frequency) coming out the right side (f_2). Where does all this "stuff" which is unwanted come from? Everywhere.

The Filter's Function

There are tons (actually, they don't weigh anything) of these invisible RF waves cruising around in the air at any moment in time at all different frequencies. These waves come from all of the RF transmissions taking place, like cellular phones, satellite communications, radar, even sunspots. All of these waves cruising around try to get into the receiver by way of the receiver antenna, and many do. Some of the signals even get past the LNA, but that's where the filter comes in. It acts like a bouncer at a nightclub letting all of the "acceptable" signals in and turning away all of those other "loser" signals. Instead of selecting people by attractiveness or wealth, the filter selects signals by their frequency.

In an ideal (and simplified) world, when the filter gets done doing its thing, the only signal still standing is the exact signal desired. Of course the world is not ideal, which is why you will often see several filters in both the transmitter and receiver.

It is simple enough to understand what the filter's purpose is in a receiver, but why is one needed in a transmitter? As you will soon learn, there is an evil component in all RF systems known as a mixer. And what this evil mixer does, (among other things), is inject unwanted signals (at unwanted frequencies) into the signal to be transmitted. But alas, the transmitter gets the last laugh, because just before the signal gets amplified by the HPA on its way out the antenna, a filter is used to eliminate all of those unwanted signals the evil mixer injected into the original signal in the first place. Ha ha ha ha ha.

The Role of the FCC

In most cases, the filter on the transmit side is required by the Federal Communications Commission (FCC). When someone is given permission to transmit a signal at a particular frequency, they are prohibited from transmitting at any other frequency, for fear it will mess up someone else's signal. The transmit filter makes sure none of these "illegal" signals ever leave the transmitter.

Did You Know?

The FCC, which has the power to allocate all airborne transmission in the U.S., actually gave away—for free—the right to the cellular frequency bands by way of lottery many years ago. After discovering that this little ploy netted the U.S. Government exactly zero dollars, they wised up. All rights to wireless transmission since then have been auctioned off to the highest bidder. Cha ching.

Filter Types

There are so many different filters that someone could write an entire book on the subject, which probably explains why there are entire books on the subject. But all filters, no matter how they are constructed, fall into one of four categories, as detailed in Table 3–2.

Table 3–2 Different Filter Types

Filter Types	Explanation
Low pass	Allows all frequencies below a certain frequency to pass while rejecting all others. It is like letting only short people into the bar.
High pass	The opposite of a low pass.

Table 3–2   Different Filter Types (Continued)

Filter Types	Explanation
Bandpass	Allows all frequencies between two specific frequencies to pass while rejecting all others. It is like letting only people between 5'10" and 6'2" into the bar. It is also called a notch filter.
Band reject	The opposite of bandpass.

Several filters are shown in Figure 3–14. Notice all the different shapes and sizes (how pretty!). Filters share the same common frequency property as all other RF stuff: the higher the frequency, the smaller the filter.

Filter Performance

Frequency Response

Generally speaking, filters are passive devices and therefore do not require a power supply. In fact, filters operate by varying their insertion loss as a function of frequency (see Figure 3–15). Figure 3–15 is known as the *frequency response* of the filter. (Could it be called anything else?) Every filter has a frequency response, which is all that is required to describe the filter's performance. Figure 3–15 shows the frequency response of a bandpass filter. With frequencies less than point A and greater than point B, the insertion loss is high. High insertion loss for a filter might be 30 dB, which means at those frequencies, the filter wipes out 99.9% of the RF signal. Conversely, frequencies between points A and B experience a low insertion loss. Low insertion loss might be one dB, which only wipes out about 20% of the signal.

Referring once again to Figure 3–15, the frequencies between points A and B are known collectively as the *passband*, because the filter allows frequencies in this band to pass on through. Likewise, the frequencies outside of the points A and B are collectively known as the *stopband*.

Figure 3–14 Filters. *Courtesy of K&L Microwave, Inc.*

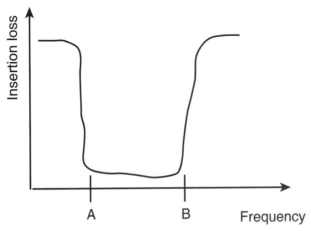

Figure 3–15 A band pass filter's frequency response.

Special Filters

Duplexers

You may hear the word *duplexer* (or *diplexer*), which is a fancy device that combines two filters into a single component. These are mostly used in conjunction with basestation antennas. By combining both the transmitter and receiver filters into the same device, the same antenna can be used for transmitting and receiving, thereby reducing the number of antennas required at the basestation. If a duplexer combines two filters in a single device, how many filters do you suppose get combined in a *triplexer*?

SAW Filters

There is one last type of filter you should be aware of, the *saw filter*, and no, it is not made out of the wood cutting tool. "Saw" stands for surface acoustic wave, which is a fancy way of saying sound wave. Remember that RF devices get bigger as the frequency gets smaller, and below a certain frequency standard RF filters become prohibitively large. One day some bright RF engineer discovered that if the RF signal is first converted into a sound signal, the components required to filter this "acoustic" wave are much smaller, which is how saw filters work. First, they convert the RF signal into a sound signal, then they filter the sound signal, and finally, they convert the sound signal back to an RF signal. Saw filters are used for very low frequency filtering. (Aren't you glad you know that?)

One last thing needs to be mentioned about filters in particular, and passive devices in general. Amplifiers aren't the only components which have a one dB compression point (P_1dB) and an third order intercept point (Ip3). Passive components, like filters as well as others, also have these parameters. In the case of passive components, these two parameters do not measure how much power the components put out (they don't—they're passive), they measure how much power the components can handle without distorting the signal. You can imagine that if a very large signal is put into a small filter, something bad will happen. In fact the "bad" thing which happens is signal distortion, which is any *unintended* change in a signal's size or shape. Of course, if the signal becomes much too big for the filter, the filter might catch on fire, which is also a form of signal distortion.

MIXERS ....

Block Diagram

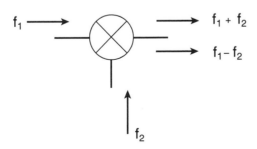

Figure 3–16 Block diagram of a mixer.

Ah, the evil *mixer*. The mathematics and physics underlying the functioning of a mixer (see Figure 3–16) are so complex, a spreadsheet is required to describe it. Fortunately, it is easy to explain conceptually.

The Mixer's Function

The Mathematics

The purpose of a mixer is to change the frequency of a signal while hopefully keeping everything else about the signal the same. Visually, one signal enters the mixer at the left side at one particular frequency (f_1), while another signal enters the bottom of the mixer at a second frequency (f_2), and what comes out of the right side are two different signals. One signal has a frequency equal to the sum of the two other frequencies ($f_1 + f_2$) and the second signal has a frequency equal to the difference between the other two frequencies ($f_1 - f_2$). A simple example will clear everything up (see Example 3–1).

This raises three questions. 1) Why does a signal's frequency need to be changed? 2) How does the fact that there are now two signals get resolved? 3) What makes mixers evil?

Example 3–1 Mixer mathematics.

> Two signals are going into a mixer. One signal has a frequency of 500 MHz and the other signal has a frequency of 400 MHz. What are the frequencies of the two signals coming out of the mixer?
>
> The first frequency can be calculated by adding the two numbers.
>
> $$500 \text{ MHz} + 400 \text{ MHz} = 900 \text{ MHz}$$
>
> The second frequency can be calculated by subtracting the two numbers.
>
> $$500 \text{ MHz} - 400 \text{ MHz} = 100 \text{ MHz}$$
>
> The two signals coming out of the mixer have frequencies of 900 MHz and 100 MHz.

Changing Frequencies

First, a signal's frequency must be changed because the signals which you and I encounter in everyday life are at different frequencies from the signals used to carry information over the air. For instance, when you speak you create sound waves in the neighborhood of 2 kHz (2000 Hertz). However, if you hope to talk on a cellular phone, the frequency of your voice (2 kHz) needs to be changed to the frequency used in cellular communications (900 MHz). In order to change the frequency of a human voice to that of the cellular carrier, one or more mixers is required.

Second, the two signals coming out of the mixer are dealt with by getting rid of the unwanted one. In the example above, if the desired signal is the 900 MHz signal, then the 100 MHz signal is eliminated. Now for the Final Jeopardy question of the day, how is the 100 MHz signal eliminated? Do do do do do do do, do do do do doo-da do do do do. With a filter, which is why there is always a filter right after a mixer, because the mixer puts out two signals and the filter gets rid of the one that isn't needed. This stuff all makes sense, if you give it a chance.

And finally, why are mixers evil? If mixers worked exactly as described above they wouldn't be evil. As you have already learned, in the world of RF, things aren't that simple. In reality, when two signals are fed into a mixer what comes out is not just two nice clean signals. Dozens of signals come out, at all different frequencies, which drive RF engineers crazy. (Come to think of it, that is one of the mixer's greatest benefits.) These unwanted signals are loosely referred to in engineering parlance as *noise*. Noise in an RF system is either a signal at a frequency which is unwanted, or an imperfection in the RF signal which is wanted. Mixers are notorious for injecting noise into RF systems, which is another reason why they are followed by a filter.

Other Names for Mixers

It needs to be pointed out that mixers are sometimes referred to as *upconverters* or *downconverters*. If the mixer is part of a receiver, then it is a downconverter. If it is part of the transmitter, well you can figure out the rest.

How Mixers Work

Three Ports

In an effort to expand your already vast RF vocabulary, the two inputs and one output (called ports) in a mixer are referred to as the RF, LO, and IF. The RF is the higher frequency signal which was previously referred to as the carrier (900 MHz in the previous example). The IF, or *intermediate frequency*, is the lower frequency signal, and the LO will be explained in the next chapter. As you might suspect, the RF, IF, and LO ports have very limited frequency ranges over which they work. Trying to operate a mixer outside one of its ports' frequency range will result in poor electrical performance. And, just like every other RF component, the wider the frequency range of the three ports, the more the mixer costs and the worse its performance is. Every attempt is made by RF engineers designing with mixers to choose the ones with the narrowest possible frequency ranges which will accomplish the task. A typical mixer is shown in Figure 3–17 (not much to look at). Make a note that the mixer does, in fact, have three ports.

There are both active mixers and passive mixers, but if the truth be told, 95% of all mixers used are passive. While active mixers do have gain, which is generally a good thing, the rest of the active mixer's performance parameters stink, so hardly anyone uses them.

Conversion Loss

Like all passive components, passive mixers exhibit insertion loss. Of course, RF engineers do not call it insertion loss, which would be too easy. Insertion loss in a mixer is called *conversion loss* (CL), just to be different. Conversion loss is one of the two most important parameters of a passive mixer. The lower the CL, the better. The other key parameter of a passive mixer is noise figure (NF). (Remember noise figure?) You thought only amplifiers have an NF. Not true. And just like LNAs, the lower the NF in a mixer, the better. Also, as indicated above, the wider the frequency ranges of the RF, IF, and LO ports, the worse will be the CL and the NF, and if you can understand this sentence with all its acronyms, you have truly grasped mixer terminology.

Figure 3–17 A mixer. *Courtesy of Mini-Circuits*

Mixer Configurations

Two-Stage Mixers

Here is one last attempt to complicate things. If there are two mixers in a transmitter or receiver, which is usually the case, the signal between them is the IF and the lowest frequency signal is referred to as the *baseband* signal (see Figure 3–18).

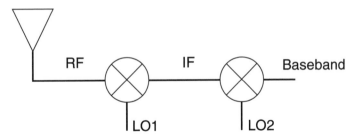

Figure 3–18 Block diagram of a two-stage mixer in a receiver.

Note that the baseband is just a lower frequency version of the RF signal. It still has the "information" signal riding on top of it. A complete receiver can be thought of as performing two functions. The first function is to lower the frequency of the carrier, and the second function is to strip off the "information" signal from the baseband signal. The second function is discussed in more detail in the section on Modulation. Of course, both of these steps also happen in the transmitter, only in the opposite order.

Did You Know?

When a receiver uses two mixers in a row, as shown in Figure 3–18, it is referred to as a superheterodyne receiver. Knowing that, plus two nickels, will get you a dime.

Mixer Types

Just to mention in passing, you should know that mixers come in three flavors: single-ended, double-balanced, and triple-balanced. These distinctions have to do with how the mixers are built internally and, for the sake of this book, have no effect on a mixer's function. All this is a long-winded way of saying when you hear any of the mixer descriptions mentioned above, ignore them and just think to yourself, mixer.

Frequency Doublers

There is another component which is closely related to the mixer: the *frequency doubler*. At the risk of insulting you, the output frequency of a frequency doubler is twice that of its input. Remember how mixers produce all sorts of unwanted signals at different frequencies? Frequency doublers use this behavior to double a signals' frequency. Enough said.

SOURCES ....

Block Diagram

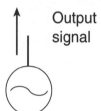

Output
signal

Figure 3–19 Block diagram of an oscillator.

The last of the major building blocks is called a source or an *oscillator* (see Figure 3–19). An oscillator which provides one of the inputs to a mixer is referred to as a *local oscillator* or LO. (I guess this is to distinguish it from a remote oscillator, which is located on Venus.) Now you know what the LO port in a mixer does: it gets connected to an oscillator.

How Oscillators Work

While the actual workings of an oscillator is somewhat involved, it is very simple to understand conceptually. A power supply is connected and, in an ideal world, out comes a perfect sine wave signal at a predetermined frequency. (That is why there is a little sine wave inside the circle.) Needless to say, all oscillators are active devices.

Oscillators are where the RF comes from in the first place. They are the "source" of the RF. Visually, it is simply a sine wave signal coming out the top of the oscillator, as shown in Figure 3–19. Several-surface mount oscillators used in today's wireless systems are shown in Figure 3–20. Notice how small they are.

Did You Know?

Almost every solid object that exists has what's known as a self-resonant frequency. What that means is if you can excite the material with electrical energy (or by tickling it), the material will actually produce a sine wave! No kidding.

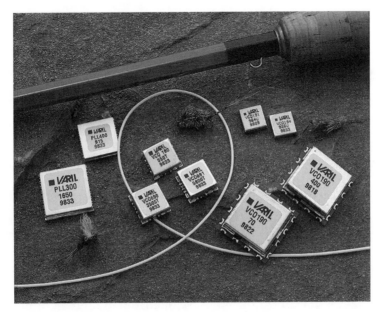

Figure 3–20 Surface-mount oscillators. *Courtesy of Varl-L Company, Inc.*

Different Kinds of Oscillators

There are many different oscillator types which make up an alphabet soup of acronyms, a selection of which is detailed in Table 3–3. Every one of these oscillators has the same objective: to provide the most perfect sine wave under the given conditions (temperature, frequency, etc.). It is imperfections in the sine wave that cause problems and require the use of additional filters.

Table 3–3 Types of Oscillators

Acronym	Oscillator	Use
DRO	Dielectric Resonator Oscillator	Accurate, high frequency
DTO	Dielectrically Tuned Oscillator	Variable DRO
OCXO	Oven-Controlled XO	Accurate, with a built-in oven
SAW	Standing Acoustic Wave	Low frequency
TCXO	Temperature-Compensated XO	Accurate over temperature
VCO	Voltage-Controlled Oscillator	Variable frequency
VCXO	Voltage-Controlled XO	Very accurate and variable
XO	Crystal Oscillator	Very accurate
YIG	Yttrium-Iron-Garnet	Accurate, very high frequency

The Reason for the Different Oscillators

The reason for all the different oscillators comes down to how "perfect" the sine wave must be. Obviously, the more perfect the sine wave, the more the oscillator is going to cost. The actual sine wave requirement is dictated by the system's requirements. For instance, digital wireless communication systems, like the newer cellular phones, require a more perfect sine wave from their LO than the communication systems of FM radio stations. Imperfections in the LO's sine wave show up as noise in the system and degrade the system's performance.

What Distinguishes Them

Inside the oscillator, the thing which determines the actual frequency and "perfectness" of the sine wave is just some small piece of material like ceramic or crystal. The exact frequency is determined by the composition and size of the material, and you should know by now that the higher the required frequency, the smaller the given piece of material will be.

There is actually a type of oscillator called a YIG (rhymes with pig) oscillator. YIG stands for Yttrium-Iron-Garnet which is a metallurgical compound that just happens to produce an incredibly perfect sine wave. How some RF engineer stumbled onto this little tidbit of information is beyond me.

How the Frequency is Determined

What frequency should the oscillator be? To answer this question, you have to go back to the operation of a mixer. A mixer adds and subtracts frequencies, which in the case of a transmitter is used to raise the frequency of the RF signal before shooting it out the antenna. In this case, the mixer is used to add two frequencies together (rather than subtract them). If the signal going into the mixer (IF) is 400 MHz and the signal we want out (RF) is 900 MHz, what must we make the frequency of the LO? I will wait for you to get your calculator. The answer is 500 MHz. Of course, the mixer gives two frequencies and the unwanted one (100 MHz) is eliminated with a filter, but you already knew that.

A Special Oscillator—The VCO

A special subset of oscillators is known collectively as *voltage-controlled oscillators* or VCOs. A VCO is an oscillator which can vary the frequency of its output sine wave in response to a change in input voltage. A block diagram of a VCO is shown in Figure 3–21.

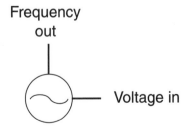

Figure 3–21 Block diagram of a VCO.

How They Work

As the voltage applied to the VCO goes up, the output frequency of the VCO goes up and vice versa. Unlike oscillators with a single fixed frequency, VCOs have a range of frequencies over which they operate. All the same rules apply to VCOs: the wider the frequency range, the more they cost, and the poorer their performance. In this case, poor performance means imperfections in the sine wave. When RF engineers design a system which requires a VCO, they choose one with a wide enough frequency range to accommodate their requirements, but no wider.

Where are VCOs used in RF systems? As you will learn later in the section on modulation, there is a type of modulation called *frequency modulation*, or FM, which is the modulation used in FM radio signals (duh). Frequency modulation works by taking the information to be transmitted wirelessly and "imprinting" it onto the RF carrier by varying the RF carrier's frequency. What device do you suppose the RF system uses to vary the RF carrier's frequency? Hint: look at Figure 3–21.

Synthesizers

The Use of Feedback

There is another type of device related to the oscillator known as a *synthesizer*. In some circumstances the sine wave coming out of an normal oscillator is just not perfect enough. Eventually, RF engineers discovered that if an oscillator is combined with a bunch of other electronic circuitry, and it utilizes something known as *feedback*, it can make the sine wave even more perfect, which is what a synthesizer is: an oscillator plus some other circuitry which employs feedback to make a more perfect sine wave.

Phase-Locked Loops

Feedback, in any electrical system, is nothing more than sensing the output of some component and, if it is not exactly the way it should be, changing the input to make it so. That is basically how synthesizers work—by sensing the output of an oscillator and, if the sine wave isn't perfect enough, making a slight modification to something inside the oscillator to improve it. When synthesizers perform this feedback activity they are sometimes referred to as *phase-locked loops* or PLLs. (Apparently the word synthesizer is just too simple.)

Real life synthesizers can become pretty sophisticated and quite costly. They also perform many more functions than just simple feedback. One of the functions a synthesizer can perform is frequency programmability. A programmable synthesizer is like a box with several different oscillators inside, all at different frequencies. The system can then select which frequency the synthesizer puts out, and in this way, the synthesizer can instantaneously switch between different frequencies. The ability to instantaneously switch between different frequencies is useful in secure military communications, as well as the newest digital wireless communication technologies.

A QUICK REVIEW ....

To quickly review all that has been covered to this point, I will follow an RF signal through the general transmitter and receiver block diagrams introduced in Figures 3–2 and 3–1, repeated here for convenience.

Transmitter Block Diagram

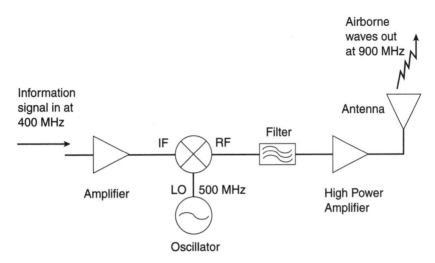

Figure 3–22 Transmitter block diagram.

Receiver Block Diagram

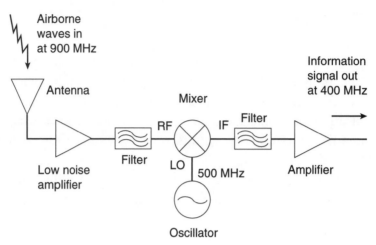

Figure 3–23 Receiver block diagram.

Review

Transmitter

Starting with the transmitter, a power supply is connected to the oscillator and out comes a perfect sine wave (hopefully) at 500 MHz. Next, another signal is injected, which is already carrying the information to be transmitted, at 400 MHz, as shown in the figure. The injected 400 MHz signal first gets amplified, because it probably isn't big enough for the mixer to use as is. In this case, the mixer is an upconverter. Out of the mixer comes two signals (sum and difference) at 900 MHz and 100 MHz and, since this is transmitting, the lower frequency one is eliminated with the ensuing filter. Finally, the signal gets amplified before it gets shoved into the antenna (as current on a conductor) and comes out as an invisible wave traveling through the air. Voila!

Antenna

If the antenna is an omnidirectional antenna, then the transmitted signal is traveling all over the place and, if the signal is strong enough and there are no obstructions, the signal will find its way into the intended receiver antenna. Just as a note: the signal also finds its way into a bunch of unintended antennas, like a neighbor's cellular phone. In fact, the signal makes it all the way through the unintended receiver, but that's where it stops, as the digital signal processor (DSP) inside the cellular phone knows to ignore the unintended signals. How it does that is the subject of my next book, *The Essential Guide to DSP*. (If curiosity is killing you, you can get a [very] brief overview of one way that it's done in the section on Spread Spectrum, in the chapter on Fixed Wireless Applications.)

Receiver

At this point, the intended receiver antenna turns the invisible wave into a current on a conductor. The signal is very weak from absorption (remember absorption?), and before it can be of any use, it needs to be made bigger (amplified). So it gets sent through the LNA, after which it is big enough to "see," then the filter eliminates all of the unwanted signals (noise) that made it through the antenna.

It is now time to recover the original information signal at 400 MHz by subtracting out 500 MHz from the 900 MHz signal. This is done by sending the signal through another mixer (downconverter) which is fed by an oscillator at the same exact frequency as the one in the transmitter, 500 MHz. Out of this mixer also comes two signals (sum and difference), one at 1400 MHz and the other 400 MHz, and this time the higher frequency signal is eliminated with a filter. And, finally, because the signal has just been through hell, it gets a little boost with a final amplifier. The original 400 MHz information signal just moved from one point to another *wirelessly*. Ain't life wonderful?

Did You Know?

For a wireless signal to be properly received, it does not need to be very powerful. Because of all the absorption in a wireless communication system, the received signal is usually on the order of a millionth of a watt (called a microwatt). It's invisible, it's infinitesimal, and yet it's still useful. I love RF.

4

Other Components

:::

There are many other components used in RF systems beyond the five basic ones covered in the previous chapter. Some of these components are very simple to understand while others are more complex. Most of these other components exist to accomplish one of two objectives. They either send the RF signal in a different direction—or in multiple directions—or they change the size or shape of the signal. All of these "other" components are used in RF systems to effectively implement wireless communications, keeping in mind that the objective at any moment in time is to have a perfect sine wave, of the exact size required, at only one frequency.

This chapter covers nine more components, and their derivatives, used in RF systems. Switches, dividers, combiners, couplers, circulators, and isolators all reroute the RF signal in one or more directions within the system. A major design objective for these components is to minimize insertion loss while rerouting the signal. Attenuators, transformers, and detectors, on the other hand, change the size and/or nature of the RF signal while keeping its shape unchanged. And, like the components covered in the previous chapter, each of these other components can be manufactured to optimize one or two key parameters. At least one example is given where each of these is used in a wireless system.

Unlike the five components covered in Chapter 3, these listed here tend to be manufactured by fewer companies, since they are used less frequently.

This offers smaller manufacturers an opportunity to carve out small, but profitable, niches producing these devices.

There are other, more esoteric, components used in RF that are outside the scope of this book. (If you really want to learn about them, get an engineering degree.) The goal of this chapter is to give you an appreciation for how the complexity of an RF circuit can grow beyond that of the five basic components used in a transmitter and receiver.

SWITCHES ....

Block Diagram

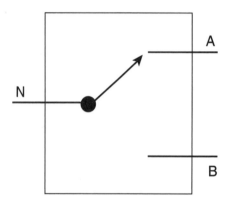

Figure 4–1   Block diagram of a single pole, double throw switch.

Switch Function and Performance

Function

Switches do what you think they do: they change the path which the RF signal is on, just like a switch on a train track. Referring to Figure 4–1, an RF signal cruising down "track" N is headed to track A, unless of course the path is switched to track B at the last minute. One interesting thing to note is that some switches work in both directions. Any component that works equally well in both directions is conveniently referred to as *bidirectional*. If the switch in Figure 4–1 is bidirectional, then two trains (RF signals) could be coming down tracks A and B at the same time, but only the one whose path is connected to N will get through. All switches are active devices (i.e.. they require some sort of power supply to function properly).

Performance

There are two key performance parameters which RF engineers look for when designing with RF switches. The first performance parameter of importance is loss. Because they are so fickle, RF switches just happen to have two different kinds of loss. In the case of Figure 4–1, an RF signal going from N to A will only experience a little bit of loss. The path from N to A is the low loss path and the loss the RF signal experiences is called insertion loss (remember insertion loss?). Insertion loss in the (closed) low loss path of an RF switch is 1 dB or less. On the other hand, if the signal at N tries to make its way to B it will not make it because the path from N to B is open and is therefore a high loss path. You may think that the open path also has insertion loss (only much higher than the closed path), and you are right. RF engineers being who they are, however, felt the need to call this "higher" insertion loss in the open path *isolation*. Isolation in a switch can be thought of as the insertion loss of the open path. Isolation in an RF switch depends on a lot of things, but the minimum useful isolation is about 20 dB.

In almost every case, RF engineers try to design switches with the lowest possible insertion loss and the highest possible isolation. And just like everything else in RF, RF switches can be made with super low insertion loss and/or super high isolation (for a price).

The other important performance parameter is switching speed, which is a measure of how long it takes for the switch to go from one position to another In general, RF engineers want the fastest possible switching speed, for the price, given the type of switch they are using.

Types of Switches

Electromechanical Switches

There are two basic types of switches in RF systems: electromechanical and solid state. Electromechanical switches are similar to the wall switch which controls a dining room light. In electromechanical switches, a control signal causes the contact to physically change positions during the switching process. The advantage to electromechanical switches is that they can handle high power RF signals because their insertion loss is very low and their isolation is very high. For this reason, they are quite often used in RF test equipment. In contrast, everything else about electromechanical switches is bad. They are big and heavy, they are slow in switching, and they cost a lot. (Other than that, they're terrific.) Switching speed for an electromechanical switch is in the order of milliseconds (thousandths of a second), which is an eternity in the RF world. Three electromechanical switches are shown in Figure 4–2.

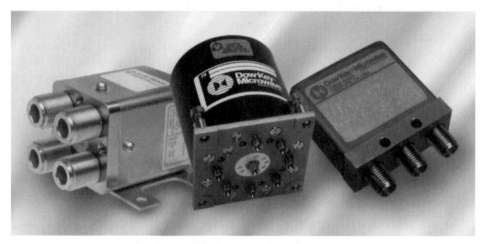

Figure 4–2   Electromechanical switches. *Courtesy of Dow-Key Microwave Corp.*

Solid State Switches

The other type of switch is solid state, which means that at the heart of the switch is some kind of semiconductor device. Unlike electromechanical switches, nothing inside solid state switches actually moves when they switch. This makes them very fast, although they cannot handle the large signals electromechanical switches can. Switching time for solid state switches is in the order of nanoseconds (billionths of a second), which is fast by anybody's measure. A solid state switch is shown in Figure 4–3. Solid state switches are either made from diodes or transistors, which you will learn about in the section on Semiconductors in Chapter 5. Why two choices? Diode switches have lower insertion loss, while switches made from transistors are faster.

Figure 4–3   A solid state switch. *Courtesy of JFW Industries, Inc.*

Poles and Throws

All RF switches come in different flavors categorized by their number of *poles* and *throws*. (It sounds like an Olympic event.) Referring to Figure 4–1, the big dot in the middle of the switch is known as a pole. The pole is the thing to which the "moving" part of the switch is hinged. A switch can have one or more poles. In essence, each pole represents a separate switch within the switch, but different poles within a single switch are not independent. They all switch at the same time.

Throws are all the different positions which the switch can switch to. In Figure 4–1, the switch can be "thrown" to two different positions, A and B, and this switch is therefore a two-throw switch. In fact, the switch in Figure 4–1 is referred to as a single-pole, double-throw switch. A switch can have any (practical) number of throws. A ten-throw switch will have ten different positions it can switch to, labeled A through J. A block diagram of a double-pole, double-throw (DPDT) switch is shown in Figure 4–4. Notice it has two poles (big dots) and each pole has two throws (positions). Ergo double pole, double throw.

Here is an interesting question. If a double-pole, double-throw switch is abbreviated DPDT, how is a single-pole, double-throw switch, like the one shown in Figure 4–1, abbreviated? SPDT. Here is a tricky one. How is a single-pole, four-throw switch abbreviated? SP4T. I think I have beaten this to death, and will therefore assume you can figure out any switch abbreviation you are likely to encounter for the rest of your life, for whatever that's worth.

Did You Know?

> There is actually a type of RF switch called a single-pole, *single-*throw (SPST), which means the switch has one input (the pole) and only *one* output (the throw). This invites the question, when the SPST switch is not connected to its one output and an RF signal is applied to the input, where does the signal go? The signal gets reflected, which is why SPST switches are only used in very low power applications.

System Use

Where is a switch used in a RF system? Suppose a cellular phone wants to use its antenna for both transmitting and receiving. The phone could utilize a T/R switch, where the antenna is connected to the N path, the receiver to the A path, and the transmitter to the B path, as shown in Figure 4–5. Furthermore, the antenna could be made to switch to the receiver path every time a

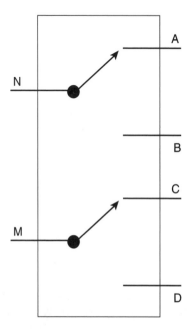

Figure 4–4 Block diagram of a double-pole, double-throw switch.

signal is coming in (the other person is talking), and it could be made to switch to the transmitter every time a signal is going out (you are talking). Not only would that work very well and eliminate the need for a second antenna, but that is precisely how many cellular phones work.

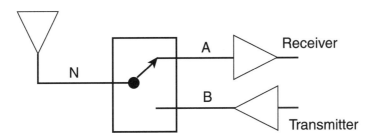

Figure 4–5 *A T/R switch between an antenna, a transmitter, and a receiver.*

Any switch which is connected to both a transmitter and receiver, like the one shown in Figure 4–5, is conveniently referred to as a transmit-receive switch, or T/R switch for short.

ATTENUATORS...

Block Diagram

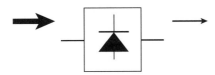

Figure 4–6 Block diagram of a generic attenuator.

The Attenuator's Function

Think of *attenuators* as anti-amplifiers. A block diagram of a generic attenuator is shown in Figure 4–6. As hard as it is to believe, sometimes in a wireless system the darn signal is just too big, which is where attenuators come in. They make a signal smaller by attenuating it. You may recall from an earlier chapter that attenuation is the result of insertion loss. Attenuation and insertion loss mean the exact same thing. Attenuators allow RF engineers to install a known amount of insertion loss into a circuit.

Visually, a big signal enters the attenuator on the left side and leaves as a smaller signal on the right. Where does the rest of the signal go? You should know that by now: heat, which is why attenuators always come with a maximum power rating. It refers to the greatest amount of RF input power the attenuator can handle without melting. Attenuators can also be represented by the block diagram shown in Figure 4–7.

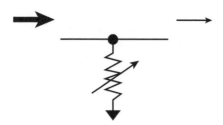

Figure 4–7   Alternative block diagram of a generic attenuator.

To demonstrate the complex nature of the average RF engineer, there are actually some RF systems in which an amplifier is immediately followed by an attenuator. Talk about indecision. They can't decide whether they want the signal bigger or smaller. There are actually good electrical reasons for doing this, but the explanation is way beyond what you need, and besides, it's just easier to think of RF engineers as complex.

Types of Attenuators

Fixed Attenuators

Attenuators fall into two categories: *fixed* and *variable*. Fixed attenuators, as the name implies, cause the signal to experience a fixed amount of loss, measured in dB. Sometimes fixed attenuators are referred to as *pads*. A typical fixed attenuator might exhibit 3 dB of insertion loss and is therefore referred to as a 3 dB pad. In this case, the signal coming out is half as big as the one going in. (Remember –3 dB is the same as dividing by 2.) A couple of fixed *coaxial* attenuators are shown in Figure 4–8. Notice that they look just like cylindrical hunk of metal, which is essentially what they are. Fixed attenuators are passive devices.

Figure 4–8 Fixed coaxial attenuators. *Courtesy of JFW Industries, Inc.*

Voltage Variable Attenuators

The other kind of attenuator is called a variable attenuator. Variable attenuators allow the RF engineer to control the exact amount of attenuation (or insertion loss), at any moment in time, by the use of an external control. There are two different kinds of variable attenuators: voltage variable attenuators (VVA) and digital attenuators, both of which are active devices.

Voltage variable attenuators vary the attenuation over a specified attenuation range and are controlled by a single external control voltage. (I guess that is why they call them voltage variable attenuators.) For instance, a VVA may be specified with an attenuation range from 2 to 30 dB, which means that by varying the control voltage, any value of insertion loss from 2 dB all the way to 30 dB can be obtained. It could even be adjusted to π (Pi) attenuation (3.14 dB) if the need arose. VVAs are used where exact amounts of insertion loss are needed in the system.

Digital attenuators

The other type of variable attenuator is a digital attenuator. Unlike the VVA, which has a single input control, digital attenuators have multiple input controls, each controlling a different value of attenuation. It is easiest to think of a digital attenuator as a bunch of fixed attenuators, all in a row, which can either be switched into or out of the circuit at any time. The trick is that each subsequent "fixed" attenuator has twice the attenuation of the previous attenuator. A quick look at Figure 4–9 will clear everything up.

An RF signal enters the digital attenuator at the left and goes through four fixed attenuators before it emerges on the right. Each attenuator which the signal goes through either has the attenuation value shown if it is on, or a value of zero if it is off. Each attenuator is turned on and off with their respective control lines A, B, C, and D. In this way, the total attenuation a signal experiences can range from 0 dB, if all the attenuators are off, to 30 dB, if all the attenuators are on. Note, however, that the attenuation value does not vary continuously from 0 to 30 dB. It cannot take any value between the two extremes, but only those which can be made by adding up various combinations of the four attenuators. For instance, 20 dB of attenuation is possible (by turning off the 2 dB and the 8 dB attenuators and turning on the 4 dB and 16 dB attenuators), but, alas, π dB of attenuation is not. For that you will need a VVA.

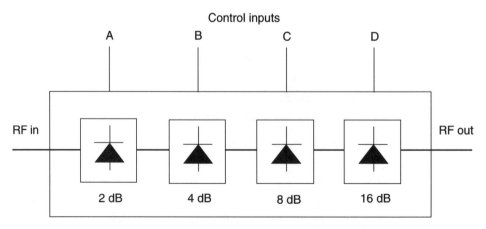

Figure 4–9   Block diagram of a digital attenuator.

Digital attenuators can be controlled by the same types of (digital) signals which run around inside a computer, which is why digital attenuators are used when RF engineers want to "program" the amount of attenuation in a circuit. A digital attenuator is shown in Figure 4–10. It cannot be seen from the outside, but inside is a very sophisticated electrical circuit. Also, compare the digital attenuator in Figure 4–10 with the fixed attenuator in Figure 4–8. They look so different, it is hard to believe they are both attenuators.

Figure 4–10 A digital attenuator. *Courtesy of Mini-Circuits.*

The key performance parameter for all types of attenuators is accuracy. Not only must the attenuation be the exact amount required—whether fixed or variable—but the attenuation must not vary over time, temperature, or anything else.

DIVIDERS AND COMBINERS ·····································

Block Diagram

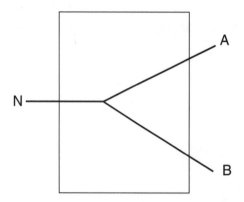

Figure 4–11 Block diagram of a two-way power divider.

The Divider's and Combiner's Function

Dividers divide. Visually, a signal goes cruising down path N (see Figure 4–11) and half the signal's power goes down path A, while the other half goes down path B. The signal gets divided in half. Its shape stays the same, but the power is reduced. Dividers are also referred to as *power dividers*.

Dividers can divide by numbers other than two. A four-way power divider has paths C and D and one quarter of the original signal's power goes down each path. Dividers always divide the input signal equally among all of the outputs.

If it were flipped over and two different signals were sent down paths A and B, then the signal on path N would become a combination of the two signals. What do you suppose RF engineers call this flipped-over divider? A *combiner*. A two-way power divider (or combiner) is shown in Figure 4–12. All power dividers and combiners are passive devices.

System Use

Why are dividers needed? Perhaps there is a wireless system which requires the use of two identical transmitters in the same place (don't ask why). Two transmitters require two of everything, including two power amplifiers, two

Figure 4–12 A two way power divider. *Courtesy of TRM, Inc.*

mixers, two sources, etc. Or do they? What if a single oscillator is used and its output is divided in half (by the divider). Then one of the signals is sent to one mixer and the other signal is sent to the other mixer. Assuming dividers are cheaper than oscillators (which they are), this reduces the cost of the hardware. Dividers are used when RF engineers want to send the same signal to more than one place in an RF system.

The key performance parameter for combiners and dividers, as well as most other passive devices, is insertion loss. The lower the insertion loss, the more of the signal which makes it through the device, which is a good thing.

COUPLERS ....

Block Diagram

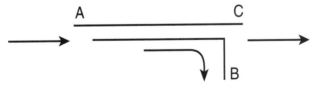

Figure 4–13 Block diagram of a directional coupler.

How Couplers Work

To understand how *couplers* function, I will use the analogy of wine tasting. Before you buy an expensive bottle of wine, you want to taste a sample. The sample does not have to be very big to know whether you are going to enjoy the whole bottle. This is how couplers work; only instead of sampling wine, they sample the RF signal.

Visually, a signal enters the coupler at point A (see Figure 4–13) and generally makes its way to point C and along its merry way somewhere else in the system. Except, as it goes from A to C, a tiny fraction of the signal is siphoned off and brought out at point B, called the sample port. The signal at point B is the sample. What can be done with the sample? Lots.

Imagine RF signals having color. Suppose the goal is to transmit an orange signal out of the antenna. A coupler could be placed just before the antenna to sample the signal before it gets radiated out. As long as the sample is orange, everything would be fine. But what if the signal which the coupler samples turns red? At that point, the sample could be used to tell some other part of the circuit to crank up the yellow, which is exactly the purpose of a coupler. A coupler samples an RF signal and yells back to some other component to change something if everything isn't just right. And if you have been paying attention, you will recognize this as an explanation of feedback. Couplers are often used as part of feedback circuits in RF systems. A directional coupler is shown in Figure 4–14. Couplers are passive devices.

Figure 4–14 A directional coupler. *Courtesy of TRM, Inc.*

Types of Couplers

Directional and Bidirectional Couplers

The coupler discussed above is referred to as a *directional coupler*, which means that it has one sample port and only works in one direction. A cousin to the directional coupler is the *bi-directional coupler*. The bi-directional coupler works in both directions and has two sample ports. (Because of the quirky nature of RF, separate sample ports are needed for waves traveling in opposite directions.)

Another way to think of directional couplers is as two-way dividers in which the power is divided unevenly: 99% of the power goes to the output and 1% goes to the sample port.

The key performance parameter for a directional coupler, in addition to insertion loss, is coupling accuracy. The amount of signal which comes out of the sample port must be known exactly and must not vary (too much) over frequency, time, temperature, or anything else, for the coupler to function properly.

Quadrature Couplers

Just when you thought you had mastered the subject of couplers, RF engineers came along and invented a whole new breed of coupler called the *quadrature* or *Lange* coupler, also referred to as a *quadrature hybrid* or *quad hybrid*. Unlike directional couplers with their sample port, quadrature couplers are almost identical to two-way power dividers. Their output power is divided evenly between the two outputs. The block diagram for a Lange coupler is shown in Figure 4–15.

There must be some difference between a quadrature coupler and a two-way power divider, right? There is, and the difference between the two concerns subtleties of RF which are way beyond the scope of this book; but as you know, that won't keep me from trying to explain it. The difference between a two-way power divider and a quadrature coupler is that in a quadrature coupler the two outputs are "out of phase." Whoa! I'm not even going to begin to explain what that means, but do you recall the balanced amplifier of a few chapters back? In a balanced amplifier, the input signal is divided in two, sent through two parallel amplifiers, and then combined

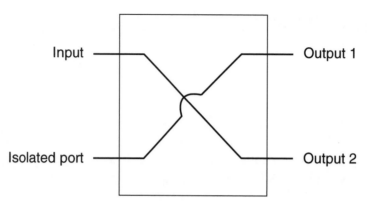

Figure 4–15 Block diagram of a Lange coupler.

again at the output. Well, that divider and combiner are, in reality, quadrature couplers. To simplify matters, quadrature couplers are used in balanced amplifiers because they improve the amplifier's match (remember match?). They are also used in digital modulation, which you will learn about in a future chapter. And just as a point of information, with reference to Figure 4–15, the isolated port does not necessarily do anything; it's just there for confusion.

CIRCULATORS AND ISOLATORS ....

Block Diagram

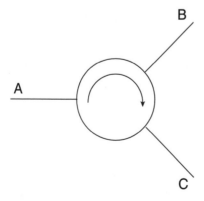

Figure 4–16 Block diagram of a circulator.

How Circulators Work

These devices are real special. You will understand *circulators* perfectly if you can picture a rotary which automobiles sometimes find themselves trapped on in cities on the east coast of the U.S. and in Europe. A rotary is a circular roadway, in the middle of a highway, with several exits on the outer periphery. All the cars travel around the circle in the same direction, and if they are lucky, they are on the outside of the circle when it is time for them to exit. A block diagram of a circulator is shown in Figure 4–16.

Circulators work the same way. All the RF signals travel in the same circular direction (see the arrow), but there is only one catch. All the RF signals have to get off at the very first exit they encounter. For instance, an RF signal getting on the circulator at point A and going clockwise around the circle must get off at point B. Those are the rules. A circulator is shown on the right side of Figure 4–17. See the three connections (called ports)?

Figure 4–17 An isolator and a circulator. *Courtesy of Nova Microwave.*

How do circulators do what they do? By building on the laws of electricity and magnetism, circulators combine magnets and a special type of material called *ferrite* to perform their magic. (Ferrite is just a material which magnetic fields really like to hang out in.) You can now impress your friends by casually dropping the word ferrite into a social conversation.

System Use

Where is a circulator used in an RF system? Think back to the example in which the switch is used to connect the antenna to the transmitter and receiver. What if the switch were replaced with a circulator as shown in Figure 4–18?

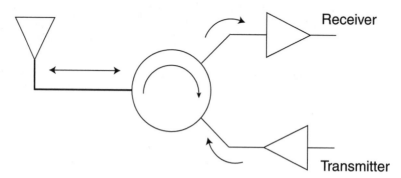

Figure 4–18 A circulator between an antenna, a receiver, and a transmitter.

Referring to Figure 4–18, following the rules of a circulator, any signal coming from the antenna gets routed by the circulator to the receiver, which is desired. Any signal coming out of the transmitter gets routed by the circulator to the antenna, which is also desired. And finally, any signal coming out of the receiver—wait a minute, there shouldn't be any signals coming *out* of the receiver. The circulator acts as kind of an intelligent switch, without actually having to switch anything. And, oh, by the way, circulators are passive devices.

Isolators

There is a particular type of circulator in which only two of the three ports are utilized, called an *isolator*. Actually, the third (unused) port is fed into a hunk of some material (called a *resistor* or load) for the sole purpose of dissipating heat. Ok, I explained my way out of the circulator, but what possible use might there be for an isolator?

Remember the discussion on match? If you recall, when two RF components are connected, some of the RF energy leaks, and, in fact, it does not leak out, but gets reflected back from where it came. Picture the point in a transmitter where the power amplifier (PA) is connected to the antenna. The power amplifier puts out a lot of power and some of it gets reflected right back to the amplifier. PAs are just like schoolyard bullies, they can dish it out but they can't take it. So while a PA may put out 50 watts, if only 2 or 3 Watts get reflected back, they go off crying to their mother amplifier. What really happens is they blow up.

Figure 4–19 shows an isolator placed between an antenna and a PA (in a transmitter). In this situation, most of the high power RF signal from the PA makes its way to the antenna and out as invisible waves. A small portion, however, gets reflected back from the antenna toward the PA. But before the reflected signal can get to the PA and cause damage, it gets rerouted by the isolator into the load where it gets dissipated harmlessly as heat. Tah dah. Isolators act to protect some RF device from reflected RF power by "isolating" it from the reflected power. An isolator is shown on the left side of Figure 4–17.

The primary performance parameter for isolators and circulators is insertion loss. RF engineers want the insertion loss to be as small as possible so that only a small amount of the signal is lost (as heat) and the majority of the signal makes it through to its intended destination.

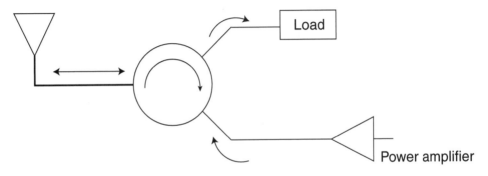

Figure 4–19 *An isolator between a power amplifier and an antenna.*

TRANSFORMERS...

Block Diagram

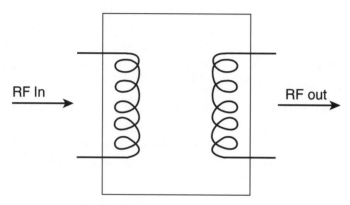

Figure 4–20 Block diagram of a transformer.

The Transformer's Function

If you recall the discussion about match, there is a standard "size" of inputs and outputs for all RF components which is 50 Ω (ohm) impedance. When the output of one device and the input of the next device are both 50 Ω (or nearly so), then the two devices are connected directly and the slight mismatch (leaking) is tolerated. However, sometimes one of the devices has an input or output which is so far from 50 Ω that trying to connect it to another device with the proper input (50 Ω) causes a horrible mismatch (leaking). What is needed in this situation is a matching circuit, and so in steps the *transformer.* It "transforms" the wrong impedance (maybe 100 Ω) into the right impedance (50 Ω), and that way the device with the wrong impedance can be utilized. A transformer is the actual device represented by the impedance matching circuit graphically depicted in Figure 2–6 on page 30. A block diagram of a transformer is shown in Figure 4–20.

Recall the garden hose analogy and imagine trying to connect two garden hoses with different size openings. A transformer is needed between the two hoses to adapt the hose with the bigger opening to that of the hose with the smaller opening, which is exactly the function of an RF transformer. Two small surface-mount transformers are shown in Figure 4–21. If you look closely, you can see the wires wrapped around like a coil, which is what the squiggly lines represent in Figure 4–20.

<u>**Did You Know?**</u>

In the world of RF, the prefix trans is used so frequently that RF engineers abbreviate it with the letter "X." Therefore, the word transformer is abbreviated as xformer, transmitter is abbreviated as xmitter, and so on. Now you can xlate from RF to English.

Impedance Ratio

As you might imagine, there are a lot of "wrong" impedances out there and so there are many different transformers. The key performance parameter of a transformer is its *impedance ratio*. The impedance ratio dictates what "wrong" impedance the transformer will make "right." If the impedance ratio is specified as 2:1, then the transformer will "transform" 100 Ω into 50 Ω. Therefore, a 2:1 transformer is used when the "wrong" impedance is 100 Ω.

There are some other uses for transformers, but they depend more on the subtleties of electronics, and for the sake of this book it is easiest to ignore them. Transformers are most often used to "transform" impedances, which is the best way to think of them.

Figure 4–21 Surface-mount transformers. *Courtesy of Coilcraft, Inc.*

DETECTORS ....

Block Diagram

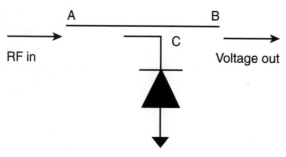

Figure 4–22 Block diagram of a detector.

The Detector's Function

A block diagram of a detector is shown in Figure 4–22, and if you think a detector looks like a cross between a coupler and attenuator, you're right, but that won't help you much. A *detector* is essentially a power-to-voltage converter. RF power enters at point A and what comes out at point B is a voltage which is proportional to the RF power.

The reason a detector is used, in place of a coupler, is that there are certain pieces of test equipment and non-RF components (like microprocessors) which cannot handle RF power directly, but can handle an electrical voltage. In these instances, the detector is used to convert the RF power to voltage, which is then sent somewhere else (either within the RF system or to a piece of test equipment) so that a decision can be made based upon it.

If you want to know what a detector looks like, look at the picture of the fixed attenuator in Figure 4–8. They look almost exactly alike. In fact, even RF engineers sometimes confuse the two, which makes for interesting circuit behavior.

5

Circuits and Signals

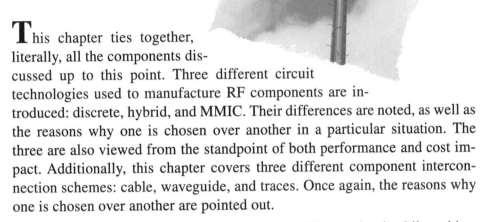

This chapter ties together,
literally, all the components discussed up to this point. Three different circuit
technologies used to manufacture RF components are in-
troduced: discrete, hybrid, and MMIC. Their differences are noted, as well as
the reasons why one is chosen over another in a particular situation. The
three are also viewed from the standpoint of both performance and cost impact. Additionally, this chapter covers three different component interconnection schemes: cable, waveguide, and traces. Once again, the reasons why
one is chosen over another are pointed out.

This chapter also introduces you to two different circuit philosophies:
lumped element and distributed. With these you will see how some RF components can actually be realized two different ways, the choice of which depends heavily on their frequency of intended use.

RF semiconductor devices are covered in detail, including the primary
materials used in RF electronics and the two main devices used in all RF
hardware: diodes and transistors. Also included is a discussion on integrated
circuits, and their advantages and disadvantages when compared to other op-
tions.

This chapter also deals with the very complicated subject of modulation, which is the term used for combining the information signal with the
carrier signal in wireless communications. The major modulation techniques
are discussed, along with some of their variations. You also will learn of the

role that digital technology has played in the evolution of the modulation schemes most prevalent in today's most sophisticated wireless systems.

SEMICONDUCTORS ....

Materials and Devices

Solid State Technology

The world of wireless communications really began to take off with the development of semiconductor technology. Another name for semiconductor technology is solid state technology. The reason it is referred to as solid state is that semiconductors are a solid material. (It also helps distinguish it from liquid state technology, in which the electrical components are made out of chocolate milk.) The other type of technology, soon to be extinct, is gaseous technology. In gaseous technology, all the electrical stuff happens in a gas. An example of a gaseous product are the old vacuum tubes found in the television sets of the sixties. Many of those old tubes were actually RF amplifiers in disguise. In those tubes, the RF signal got bigger (amplified) while it floated around in a gas in the tube.

Gas-based electrical products (tubes) are, with only a few exceptions, no longer used in RF communications. It is not that the old tubes can't do what semiconductors can—they can, it is that semiconductors have two really attractive properties which tubes do not: they can be made very small and very cheap (not to mention they don't break when they're dropped).

Silicon and Gallium Arsenide

There are two primary semiconductor materials used to manufacture RF components: *silicon* (Si) and *gallium arsenide* (GaAs), also known as "gas." In general, GaAs is used for higher frequency applications. If some RF component utilizes GaAs, chances are that silicon didn't work at the (high) frequency of intended use. When given a choice, an RF engineer will choose a silicon device over a GaAs device because it is less expensive.

There are other, more exotic materials used to make RF components in addition to silicon and GaAs. However, they are all relatively new, not widely used yet, and tend to be a combination of GaAs or Silicon and some other obscure material. So for the time being, just know that there are other materials out there.

Diodes and Transistors

There are only two basic semiconductor building blocks used in the RF world: *diodes* and *transistors*. Before you start thinking that things are pretty simple with only two basic building blocks, know that there are a lot of different kinds of diodes and transistors and they are all used for different reasons. Table 5–1 highlights the most popular diodes and transistors used in RF systems.

Table 5–1   RF Diode and Transistor Types

Diode Types	Transistor Types
PIN	MESFET
Schottky	MOSFET
Gunn	Bipolar
Impatt	HEMT & PHEMT
Tunnel	JFET
Varactor	LDMOS

Before you start feeling overwhelmed with all the different types of diodes and transistors, understand that the primary difference between them is in how they are fabricated and from what material they are made. All the diodes pretty much do the same thing, but because they are fabricated differently, they have superior electrical performance in different areas. For instance, Schottky diodes are fabricated to be fast, while PIN diodes are fabricated to handle a lot of power. The same goes for transistors. Most diode types indicated in Table 5–1 can be made of either silicon or GaAs, while the transistors are made of one material or the other, but not both.

Diodes

Diodes are used in many different components in the RF world, but they are primarily used in three components: switches, mixers, and voltage variable attenuators (VVA). (If you want to know what a diode looks like in block diagram form, it is the weird shape on the attenuator shown in Figure 4–6.) If Schottky diodes are fast and PIN diodes can handle substantial amounts of power, what diode is used if the switch needs to be fast? How about if it has to handle a lot of power?

As mentioned in Chapter 3 on sources, most oscillators utilize some sort of material to determine the actual frequency of oscillation. This technique works well for "lower" RF frequencies. For "higher" RF frequencies (greater than 10 GHz), material choice is limited and so oscillators frequently use a diode to determine the frequency of oscillation. Gunn, Tunnel, and Impatt diodes are all used to generate these "higher" RF frequencies in oscillators, especially Impatts, which are used for super high RF frequencies (greater than 100 GHz).

Varactor diodes can be thought of as "variable diodes" and are used in voltage controlled oscillators (VCO). Recall from Chapter 3 that VCOs are oscillators whose output frequency can vary over some range. Well, the reason it can vary is because it utilizes a "variable diode" (varactor) to determine its frequency. (All of this stuff really does make sense.)

Transistors

Transistors are used extensively in RF—from low noise amplifiers to high power amplifiers, to switches, attenuators, mixers, oscillators, you name it. Transistors are the workhorse of RF. Block diagrams of the two most common transistor types are shown in Figure 5–1, strictly for entertainment purposes.

Here is a great rule to remember: if there is gain, there is at least one transistor. All solid state amplifiers use transistors of one kind or another. To produce a lot of gain, amplifiers require two or more transistors.

The lowest frequency (less than 1 GHz) transistor used in RF is the MOSFET, which stands for Metal Oxide Semiconductor Field Effect Transistor. Your intuition should tell you that MOSFETs are made from silicon and they are primarily used in high power amplifiers (HPA).

Above 1 GHz, RF engineers choose between bipolar transistors and MESFETs, which stands for Metal Semiconductor Field Effect Transistor. Bi-

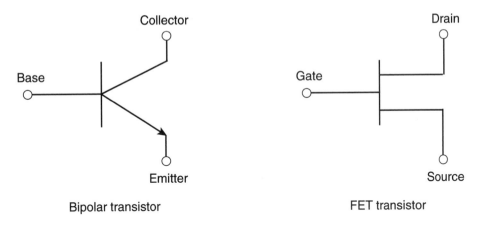

Figure 5–1   *Circuit representation of a bipolar and FET transistor.*

polar transistors are always made from silicon and MESFETs are always made from GaAs. Which transistor type is better? Well, if cost is an issue, then (silicon) bipolar transistors are the better choice because they are cheaper. If, on the other hand, the transistor needs to operate at a particularly high frequency, then the (GaAs) MESFET is the better choice. As another consideration, at frequencies where either transistor type can be used, bipolar transistors are manufactured to produce more RF power than MESFETs, while MESFETs provide a lower noise figure (NF) than bipolars. In summary, bipolars are less expensive and produce high power, while GaAs FETs cost more but work better at higher frequencies while delivering lower noise figures.

There is a new type of transistor on the block which is known as LD-MOS (pronounced 1 dee´ mäs), which stands for Laterally Diffused Metal Oxide Semiconductor. (I couldn't make this stuff up.) Some bright young RF engineer discovered that if a MOSFET is fabricated a little differently, it can be made to work at frequencies above 1 GHz. Where do you suppose these LDMOS transistors get used? If you said high power amplifiers above 1 GHz, give yourself a prize.

HEMT Transistors

There is new family of transistors, specifically designed for super high frequency applications, known as HEMT and PHEMT, which stands for High Electron Mobility Transistor and Pseudomorphic HEMT, respectively. (How many people do you suppose you would have to ask before you could find one who knows what "pseudomorphic" means?) Picture the electrons in an ordinary MESFET as cars traveling on a regular highway (speed limit: 55 MPH). HEMT transistors are nothing more than MESFETs in which the electrons have been given their own high speed autobahn. If the electrons can travel faster, then the transistor can work at higher frequencies. HEMT transistors are particularly suited to high frequency, low noise applications.

Something to note: When I say certain transistors "work" at higher frequencies and others do not, what I really mean is that certain transistors work well at higher frequencies and others perform poorly, even though technically they "work" at higher frequencies. Poor performance manifests itself as degraded electrical parameters like power, gain, and noise figure.

Integrated Circuits (MMIC)

Some clever engineers figured out awhile back that if an amplifier (or other device) needs, say, three transistors, two diodes, and a bunch of other electrical components, why not just put all of these goodies onto a single piece of semiconductor (silicon or GaAs). There are many advantages to doing this, including lower cost and smaller size. When more than one electrical device (transistor, diode, etc.) is combined onto a single piece of semiconductor, it is called an *integrated circuit* (IC).

Of course, RF engineers couldn't let their devices be called just integrated circuits for fear that people might confuse them with other integrated circuits, like the Pentium microprocessor in a PC. RF engineers complicate matters by calling their ICs *Monolithic Microwave Integrated Circuits or MMICs* (pronounced mim´iks). (Whatever.)

Most of the components covered to this point can be made as MMICs. A MMIC is not a particular device, it is a manufacturing technology used to realize particular components. For instance, a MMIC which uses a bunch of transistors to make an amplifier is called a MMIC amplifier, while a MMIC which uses a bunch of transistors to make a switch is called a MMIC switch. (You get the idea.)

MMIC Performance

If a component can be made as a MMIC, which is smaller and cheaper (per unit) than other approaches, why aren't all components made as MMICs? There are two drawbacks to MMICs. First, since they involve the semiconductor manufacturing process, they are very expensive if only a few will be needed. Therefore, MMIC technology is only used when the volume requirement is sufficient enough to justify the initial investment to develop the MMIC. Second, quite often MMICs have worse performance (on key parameters) than the same device made out of individual components. Where performance is at a premium, like low noise in a low noise amplifier or high power in a high power amplifier, the devices are made out of individual transistors (or diodes). When performance is not as critical, and cost is, the devices used are MMICs.

To quickly review, there are two main semiconductor materials used in the RF world: silicon and gallium arsenide. Silicon and gallium arsenide are used to make two basic building blocks: diodes and transistors. RF devices can be manufactured two ways: by combining individual diodes and transistors or as integrated circuits (MMICs).

Did You Know?

There is a special class of RF MMICs called ASICs, which stands for Application Specific Integrated Circuit. ASICs are nothing more than custom MMICs, designed to accomplish one specific task and usually intended for only a single customer. Because they are custom-made, ASICs must be used in high volume to justify the design expense. Cellular phones are the ideal candidate for ASICs. In fact, some people believe that to get the cost of cellular phones down even lower, in the not-too-distant future, cellular phones will have just a single component inside of them: an ASIC. I say, what's the holdup?

CIRCUIT TECHNOLOGIES ....

Lumped and Distributed Circuits

RF components are frequently made up of several different electrical components called *discrete* components. For instance, while an RF amplifier is an RF component, it is made up of several discrete electrical components like diodes, transistors, and the big three: *resistors*, *capacitors*, and *inductors*. Resistors, capacitors, and inductors are small, inexpensive passive electrical components used to shape electrical signals and are utilized in some combination in every electrical circuit.

When electrical components are combined together in a defined area to perform some prescribed function, the components are said to form a *circuit*. In the world of RF, there are two philosophies behind circuit design: *lumped element* circuits and *distributed* circuits.

Lumped element and distributed circuits both use the same semiconductor devices (transistors, diodes, and MMICs) in their designs. Where they differ is in the nature of the passive components they use, specifically the big three, as well as others like transformers and couplers.

Lumped Circuits

In lumped element circuit designs, the capacitors and inductors are real things which can be seen and touched. A sampling of "real" capacitors and inductors is shown in Figure 5–2. In lumped element designs, couplers are really just transformers. (I told you they were used for other things.)

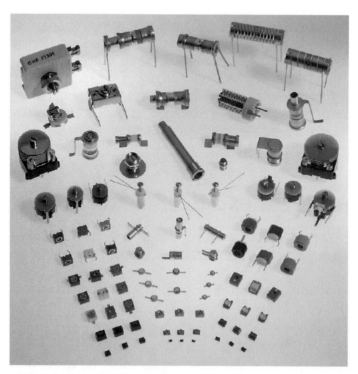

Figure 5–2   Lumped element ("real") capacitors and inductors. *Courtesy of Sprague-Goodman Electronics, Inc.*

Distributed Circuits

Distributed circuits are where things get interesting. As you recall from the introduction, signals in the RF world get around in a circuit by cruising around on a conductor which is often just a small, thin piece of metal (called a *trace*) on a printed circuit board (PCB) or other substrate. An interesting thing happens to these metal traces at RF frequencies: they begin to act as discrete components. In distributed circuits, RF engineers can shape the metal traces in very specific ways to make them behave like capacitors, inductors, transformers, and even couplers, which is why in pure distributed circuits the only "real" devices are semiconductors, the rest are just a bunch of odd-shaped metal traces. Figure 5–3 shows an example of a distributed circuit. The circuit traces in the small square area on the left side of the figure actually form a coupler, which looks quite a bit different from a lumped element (transformer) coupler (refer to Figure 4–21 in the previous chapter).

How is the choice made between circuit philosophies when designing a circuit? While both have their advantages and disadvantages, the decision is usually very simple. Remember in the RF world, the higher the frequency, the smaller things get, and vice versa. If a circuit is to operate at a "low" RF frequency, then the components will be relatively bigger. And if the compo-

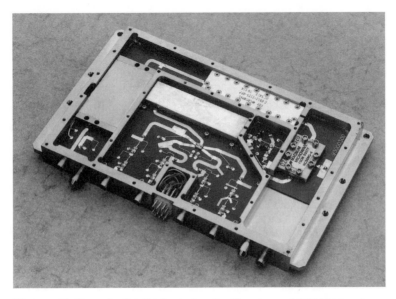

Figure 5–3   A distributed circuit. *Courtesy of JCA Technology.*

nents need to be bigger, then the size and shape of the circuit traces needed to realize the components in a distributed design become prohibitively large. All this is a long-winded way of saying, below a certain frequency, the only circuit choice is a lumped element design. Conversely, above a certain frequency, the only reasonable choice is a distributed circuit design, and in between, you flip a coin.

Discrete, Hybrid, and MMIC Circuit Choices

Once a circuit philosophy is selected (or dictated), the next choice is what circuit technology to use. Once again there is a choice to be made, this time from three different circuit technologies: discrete, hybrid (also called MIC, for microwave integrated circuit), or MMIC (microwave monolithic integrated circuit). Table 5.2 details the three choices and their respective advantages and disadvantages. An example of each type is shown in Figures 5–4a, 5–4b, and 5–4c. Figure 5–4b (the MIC) contains both packaged and bare "chip" semiconductors.

Table 5.2   Discrete, Hybrid, and MMIC Circuit Technology Comparison

Technology	Description	Advantages	Disadvantages
Discrete	Combines semiconductor devices (diodes, transistors and MMICs) and lumped passive devices as individually packaged discrete components onto a printed circuit board (PCB).	Utilizes existing discrete components, fast design time, superior performance at high power.	Takes up a lot of space, reduced performance at high frequency, expensive in large quantity.
Hybrid (MIC)	Combines both packaged and "chip" semiconductor devices (diodes, transistors, and MMICs), and passive devices (both lumped and distributed), along with metal traces onto a ceramic substrate.	Smaller and better high frequency performance than discrete, cheaper than discrete in large quantity, superior high frequency performance.	Expensive in small quantity, longer design time than discrete, more delicate handling and troubleshooting than discrete.

Table 5.2 Discrete, Hybrid, and MMIC Circuit Technology Comparison (Continued)

Technology	Description	Advantages	Disadvantages
MMIC	Combines semiconductor devices (diodes and transistors) and distributed passive devices onto a single piece of semiconductor.	Smaller than any other approach, less expensive than any other approach in high volume.	Very expensive in small quantity, very long design time, some degradation in performance compared to hybrid approach.

Figure 5–4a A discrete circuit. *Courtesy of Alpha-Industries.*

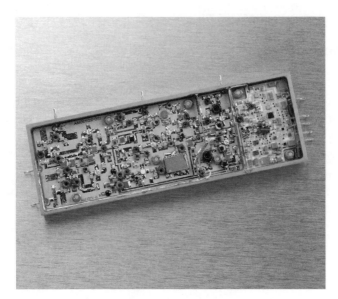

Figure 5–4b A hybrid circuit. *Courtesy of Micro Networks.*

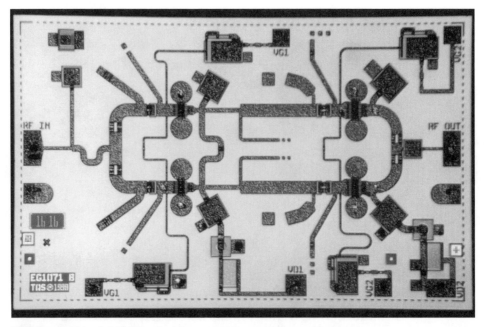

Figure 5–4c A MMIC. *Courtesy of TriQuint Semiconductor, Inc.*

The predominant way that discrete components get mounted onto RF printed circuit boards (PCB) today is by what is known as surface mount technology (SMT). In SMT, the individual components get soldered right to the surface of the PCB. Now this may seem obvious, but in the early days of electronic manufacturing, another technique called feed-through technology, was used in which the individual components were actually fed through little holes drilled in the PCB. So if nothing else, SMT saves on drill bits.

The newest MIC technology used today is called Low Temperature Co-fired Ceramic, or LTCC for short. LTCC is just like a PCB (with its multilayer traces), only it is made from ceramic instead of a plastic composite. LTCC allows the MIC to be made very small, which is ideal for use in very high frequency components.

Subassemblies

There are certain RF manufacturers who make a living by combining more than one RF component, to perform more than one RF function, into a single package. When a box of RF "stuff" performs more than one basic function, like a single mixer or a single amplifier, the box of stuff is referred to as a *subassembly*.

Sometimes a subassembly is referred to as a subsystem. Now there is no technical difference between the two descriptions, but companies selling "subsystems" have been known to fetch a higher price than those selling "subassemblies." That's marketing for you.

As an example of a subassembly, refer back to the block diagram of a receiver in Figure 3–1. A receiver has a mixer which is fed by an oscillator and followed by a filter. If some enterprising RF manufacturer thought it made good business sense, they might combine all three components (mixer, oscillator, and filter) into a single box and call it a mixer-oscillator-filter subassembly (or a mixoster?). The good news regarding subassemblies, at least as far as the manufacturer is concerned, is that because they are complicated to make, they fetch a high price. On the flip side, however, subassemblies take a long time to develop, require a lot of engineering and, because they are so specific, tend to have only a single customer. Because of this, manufacturing subassemblies is considered risky business. Of course, that doesn't keep a lot of manufacturers from trying.

Cavities

There is one final way an RF component can be manufactured. Unlike the other technologies (discrete, hybrid, and MMIC), *cavity* type components do not use conductors to carry the RF signal. Instead, RF signals move as waves inside cavity components.

A cavity circuit is some sort of hollow container made out of metal with the RF signal bouncing around on the inside. Cavity technology is a fairly old RF technology, and many different RF components can be made as cavity components, like couplers, oscillators, and even amplifiers. When an amplifier is of the cavity type, it is called a *traveling wave tube amplifier* or TWTA (or TWT for short). (It makes sense: an amplifier with a wave traveling around inside a tube-shaped cavity *should* be called a traveling wave tube amplifier!) A TWT is shown in Figure 5–5.

Cavity components are used for one reason and one reason only: high power. When RF engineers need to amplify a signal really big—bigger than any transistor can amplify it—they use a cavity amplifier (TWT). When they need to couple a high power signal or filter a high power signal, they use cavity components. The output filters of cellular basestations are (guess what?) cavity filters, because the output power of basestations is relatively high. (Cavity filters also happen to have the superior filtering characteristics required by cellular transmitters, but that's another story.)

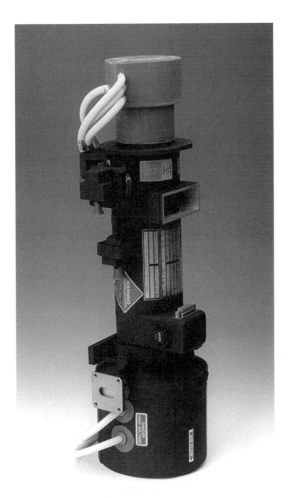

Figure 5–5   A traveling wave tube. *Courtesy of Litton Electron Devices.*

MODULATION ....

What is Modulation?

Modulation is a mathematically complex subject which is difficult to explain quantitatively because it is easy to get lost in all of the formulas. Fortunately, it is simple to visually understand, which is how it is covered here.

Earlier, I described a digital signal as "riding on the back of the RF." Modulation is the way the information signal (analog or digital) is made to ride on the back of the carrier signal (the RF). This is done by taking the RF signal and superimposing the information signal onto it. The act of superimposing the information signal onto the RF (carrier) signal is called *modulation,* and the device which does the superimposing is called a *modulator*. In RF systems, the RF first gets modulated and then sent through the transmitter and out the antenna. After the signal arrives at the receiver, the process is done in reverse. The received signal gets *demodulated* (the RF carrier gets stripped away), leaving only the information signal.

As a way to visualize modulation, think of mailing a letter as wireless communication. The envelope is the RF (the carrier) and the letter inside is the information. To get a letter (the information) from point A to point B, a letter is placed in an envelope (the signal gets modulated) and dropped into the mailbox. Once the envelope arrives, the envelope is opened (the RF is stripped away) and voila, the letter (the information) has moved from point A to point B. When something is transmitted wirelessly, two signals are sent: the RF carrier (the envelope) and the information signal (the letter). The act of combining these two is called modulation.

You will recall from Chapter 3 that the goal of every source (oscillator) is to produce a perfect sine wave, which is the RF. The reason why a perfect sine wave is needed is because modulators superimpose the information signal onto the (perfect) RF signal by making tiny modifications to it. If the RF signal is not perfect, the imperfections may be incorrectly interpreted as modifications (information), which is unwanted.

Modulators and demodulators do what they do by changing some aspect of the RF signal (a perfect sine wave) in some specific way. Technically, they aren't really considered devices or components. They are better thought of as *subsystems*, which are combinations of two or more components.

Types of Modulation

In the world of wireless communications today there are literally dozens of different types of modulation used (and more being created every day). The good news is that all forms of modulation fall into one of three general categories: *amplitude modulation* (AM), *phase modulation* (PM), and *frequency modulation* (FM), which is used to broadcast FM radio. AM and FM are older forms of modulation which have been around since the early days of wireless communication. PM is the new kid on the block and the one which is used most frequently in today's (advanced) digital wireless communication systems.

The reason AM and FM came in to being first is that the sophisticated digital chips needed to implement PM just weren't around at the beginning of wireless communication. Digital wireless communication and PM evolved as a direct result of the advances in digital semiconductor integrated circuits.

AM, FM, and PM describe the three ways in which the perfect sine wave changes as it accepts the information signal. AM changes the height of the sine wave (as time goes by), FM changes the frequency of the sine wave (as time goes by), leaving the amplitude unchanged, and PM changes the phase of successive sine waves. These changes contain the information.

Amplitude Modulation

AM changes the amplitude of the perfect sine wave RF carrier as shown in Figure 5–6. The left side of Figure 5–6 shows how an unmodulated sine wave appears. Note that the sine wave is repeated many times. The right side of Figure 5–6 shows what happens to the sine wave after it has been amplitude modulated. Notice that the sine waves are still there and that the frequency is still the same (the space between successive sine waves is unchanged), but the amplitude (height) of each successive sine wave varies. The amplitude changes (or is modulated) from sine wave to sine wave, but the frequency is unchanged. If you trace your finger over the top of the signal on the right side you will notice that it follows the path of a sine wave, which is no coincidence.

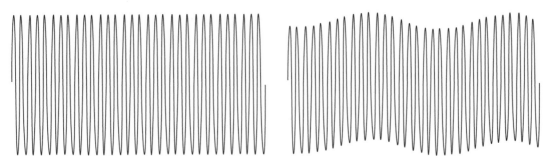

Unmodulated RF   Amplitude modulated RF

Figure 5–6   *An unmodulated and an amplitude modulated RF carrier.*

AM has been around longer than any other modulation scheme, primarily because it is easy to implement. Of course, this ease of implementation comes with a price. All RF signals pick up noise as they move around. As mentioned in Chapter 3, noise is any imperfection in the (RF carrier) sine wave. More often than not, these imperfections manifest themselves as random changes in amplitude. So when noise changes the amplitude of the RF carrier, the RF system doesn't know whether the change is intended (as a result of amplitude modulation) or unintended (as a result of noise). What all this means is that AM signals are very susceptible to being distorted by noise.

The AM depicted in Figure 5–6 is a type of "analog" AM. In analog AM, the system modulates the RF carrier with an analog signal, e.g., a sine wave. In essence, it superimposes a sine wave onto a bunch of other sine waves, as can be seen in the figure. Analog AM has been around for a long time and not much has changed—until very recently.

Binary Amplitude Shift Keying

There is a new generation of AM, which is digital in nature, known as Binary Amplitude Shift Keying (BASK). Unlike "analog" AM, which superimposes an analog (sine wave) signal onto the RF (sine wave) carrier, BASK superimposes a digital signal (like the one in Figure 1–3) onto the RF (sine wave) carrier (see Figure 5–7). Notice how the shape of the RF carrier mimics the shape of the digital signal.

BASK is less noise-sensitive than analog AM. BASK signals are still susceptible to random changes in amplitude from noise, but since the "smarts" of the RF system only have to differentiate between a "high" and a "low," slight changes in either amplitude (high or low) will not cause the system to misinterpret one as the other. BASK is used in today's digital wireless systems because it is less susceptible to noise.

Frequency Modulation

FM describes a second way a perfect sine wave can be made to vary (see Figure 5–8). Notice in this case that the amplitude remains the same (from unmodulated to modulated), but the frequency changes (the space between successive sine waves changes). This change in frequency (as time goes by)

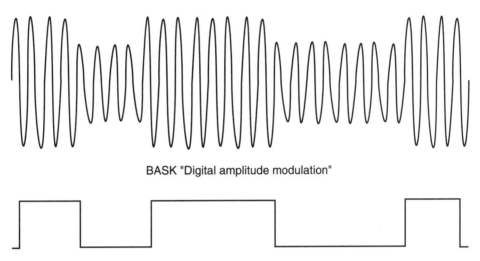

BASK "Digital amplitude modulation"

Figure 5–7   Binary Amplitude Shift Keying (BASK)

actually contains information, like a human voice on a cellular phone call. (As hard as it is to believe, it's true.)

FM is not as sensitive to noise as AM, which is why it came about. Like AM signals, FM signals are still susceptible to random changes in amplitude from noise, but since the "smarts" of the system is only looking for changes in frequency, the system disregards changes in amplitude. Before you start thinking that FM sounds like a free lunch—you should know better, there is also a type of noise which affects a signal's frequency, but that's another story.

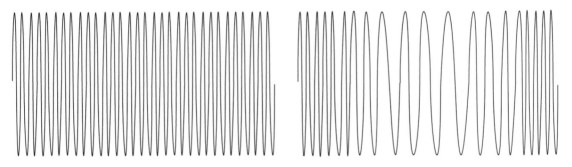

Unmodulated RF   Frequency modulated RF

Figure 5–8   *An unmodulated and a frequency modulated RF carrier.*

Phase Modulation

PM is the third way a perfect sine wave can be made to vary. PM is similar to FM in that the amplitude is unchanged while the spacing between successive sine waves changes. Much of the digital information today is modulated onto the RF carrier by way of phase modulation.

There are many different types of PM used in digital wireless communications. The reason that so many exist is that the different modulation techniques evolved as the semiconductor technology evolved. The latest and greatest PM techniques utilized today just weren't possible with the electronic components of 10 years ago. A sampling of some of the more popular PM techniques used in digital wireless communication are shown in Table 5–3.

Table 5–3   Some Common Phase Modulation Types

Acronym	Phase Modulation
MSK	Minimum shift keying
BPSK	Bi-phase shift keying
QPSK	Quadrature phase shift keying
DQPSK	Differential QPSK
GMSK	Gaussian minimum shift keying

All you really need to know about the different phase modulation techniques is that they all take information in digital form and translate it into changes in the sine wave spacing (the phase) of the RF carrier, similar to that shown in Figure 5–8.

Quadrature Amplitude Modulation

The newest form of modulation used in today's digital wireless systems is Quadrature Amplitude Modulation or QAM (pronounced kwäm). QAM is simply a combination of (digital) AM and PM. It has all the noise advantages of BASK and PM and, since each successive sine wave can be modified two ways (amplitude and phase), QAM can impart a lot of information onto each sine wave of an RF carrier.

Modulators and Demodulators

RF signals get modulated by modulators, which are fairly complex devices, but they can all be represented by a simple block diagram, as shown in Figure 5–9.

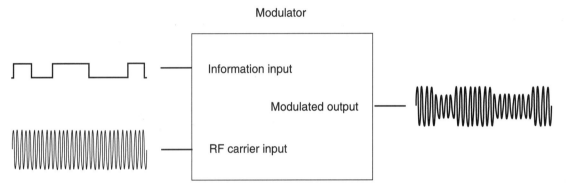

Figure 5–9   Block diagram of a modulator.

At their simplest, modulators have two inputs and one output. One input is the "information" input, which can be in analog or digital form. In Figure 5–9, the information is in digital form. The other input is the RF carrier (a perfect sine wave). When the modulator gets done doing its thing, out comes a signal which is a composite of the two signals. This is the modulated output signal, and in Figure 5–9, it is BASK modulation. And, of course, *demodulators* do the exact opposite: they take a modulated signal and break it down into an information signal and a carrier signal. After demodulation, the carrier is no longer needed and therefore it is disregarded while the information signal is sent somewhere else in the system for further use.

How do modulators and demodulators do what they do? It depends on the type of modulation of course, but it is safe to assume that there is one or more mixers involved. In terms of their location in an RF system, modulators come before the transmitter and demodulators come after the receiver (see Figures 3–1 and 3–2).

Technically, saying "QAM modulation" is redundant, because QAM modulation literally means Quadrature Amplitude Modulation modulation. The same goes for "AM modulation" and "FM modulation." But alas, it's spoken that way by convention, and because "QA modulation" just sounds too awkward.

GETTING AROUND...

Once an RF signal enters an antenna and gets transformed into a current, it needs to get around, moving from component to component. I have called this thing which carries the current a conductor, but there are several media used in the RF world to get a signal from one point to another in a receiver or in a transmitter. These media, represented by the straight lines in any RF block diagram or schematic, fall into one of three categories: cables, waveguides, and circuit traces.

Cables

Cable Construction

One way RF signals move around is through cables. The cable hooked up to the back of a VCR is an example of an RF cable, albeit an inexpensive one. RF cables are known as *coaxial cables*, which is a fancy way of saying that there is an inner conductor surrounded by an outer conductor. To help you visualize it, picture an old-style wooden pencil (think kindergarten). If it were a coaxial cable, the lead would be the center conductor, the ugly yellow paint on the outside would be the outer conductor, and the wood, which separates the two conductors, would be referred to as the—brace yourself—*dielectric* material. Dielectric is just fancy engineering talk for *insulator*, which is any material that does not conduct electricity (or carry an RF signal).

The reason for the two conductors is a simple one. The inner conductor carries the RF signal and the outer conductor, which is really a shield, is there to keep the RF signal from escaping. The reason the outer shield is needed is because the center conductor thinks it is an antenna, and it tries to radiate the RF signal it is carrying out into space. The outer conductor prevents that from happening. (Think of it as the security guard of the coaxial prison.) A variety of coaxial cables is shown in Figure 5–10.

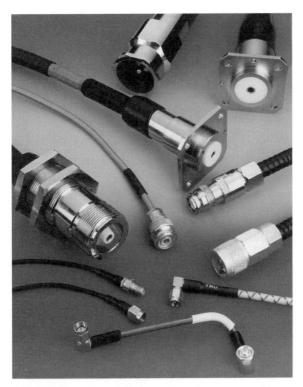

Figure 5–10 Coaxial cables. *Courtesy of Tru-Connector Corp.*

All RF coaxial cables try to accomplish the same objective: to get an RF signal from one point to another with the least amount of insertion loss possible. Of course, in this no-free-lunch world there is always a tradeoff to be made. The bigger (and heavier) the coaxial cable, the lower the insertion loss, but the more it costs and the harder it is to deal with. Big heavy cables cannot be bent around small objects, which makes them difficult to work with, not to mention incredibly heavy. Therefore, RF engineers use the smallest possible cable which has an insertion loss they can live with.

Coaxial cables are most often used as interfaces between major building blocks within an RF system. For instance, cables are frequently attached to the bottom of antennas at basestations to carry the signal from the antenna, down the tower, and into a room where the low noise amplifier (LNA) awaits.

Cable Types and Designations

Not wanting to keep things too simple, RF engineers went out and developed several different types of coaxial cables for all different occasions. The three main types of coaxial cables are differentiated by their outer layer as detailed in Table 5–4.

Table 5–4   Coaxial Cable Types

Cable type	Outer layer	Description
Flexible	Rubber coating surrounding a very thin metal shield.	Very flexible, the rubber outer coating is used as protection for the thin outer shield.
Semi-flex	Thin metal (braided) shield.	Less flexible and less durable than flexible cable, often cheaper.
Semi-rigid	Thick solid metal shield.	Less flexible, but more durable, than semi-flex.

Cables of different sizes need to be specified as such. A flexible cable with a one-half inch diameter could be called a flexible cable with a one-half inch diameter, but by now you already know that RF engineers have a way of taking perfectly simple notions and complicating them. So the cable mentioned above is referred to as RG-58. In fact, most coaxial cables are referred to as RG something or other. There are dozens of different RG numbers and unless you plan on buying coaxial cables for a living, the only thing you need to know about a cable's RG number is that the smaller the number, the larger the cable's diameter. Therefore RG-58 is bigger (and more expensive) than RG-114.

Connectors

Cables by themselves are of little use unless they are terminated with a *connector*, or more specifically, a coaxial connector. A coaxial connector is what allows one cable to be connected to another or to a component. Because of this, there are two different kinds of connectors: those intended to be attached to cables and those intended to be attached to components. Without both, it would be impossible to connect cables to components. The difference between a cable connector and a component connector can be seen in Figure 5–11. The component connectors are the ones with the four-hole flanges.

Connectors in Cable Assemblies

In the case of cables, connectors are firmly attached to the end of the cable mechanically, as well as electrically. Once connectors are attached to a cable, its referred to as a *cable assembly*. Sometimes RF engineers purchase cable assemblies and sometimes they purchase plain (bulk) cable and individual cable connectors and attach the parts themselves. Why do they choose to make their own cable assemblies rather than purchase them ready-made? When only a few cable assemblies are required, then assembling them is cheaper and faster. However, when a lot of them are required, it is best to let the pros do it.

Figure 5–11 Cable connectors and component connectors. *Courtesy of Tru-Connector Corp.*

Connector Families

Just like with cables, the goal of every connector is the same: minimum insertion loss. Yes, connectors have insertion loss, although it is tiny compared to the cable. If you think there are a lot of different cables, wait until you see how many RF connector types exist. A sampling, and I repeat a sampling, of RF coaxial connector types (called families) is shown in Table 5–5. Almost all of these connector families have connectors made for both cables and components. As a general rule, a connector of one family will *not* mate up with a connector of a different family.

Table 5–5 RF Coaxial Connector Families

SMA	SSMA
SMB	SMC
BNC	TNC
N	7–16
SC	7mm
3mm	2.4mm
1.4mm	K
SMT	SSMT
SMP	SSMP
OSP	OSSP
OSX	Type 43

Why so many different connector families? There are two reasons. First, some connector families are physically large while others are small. As mentioned before, if an inexpensive cable assembly is desired, then a cable is chosen with a small diameter, which limits the choice of connector to the available small connector families. If the cable needs to carry a high power RF signal, a large diameter cable is needed and therefore so is a large connector.

The second reason for all the connector families is one of evolution. Connector designers are constantly trying to improve connectors, either by lowering the insertion loss or making the connector easier to use. Each time they make a significant improvement to an existing connector type, a whole new family of connectors is born. All of these connector families just represent improvements in connector technology over time.

Adapters

An interesting thing happens as a result of all these different connector families. Sometimes RF engineers are forced to connect a cable with a connector from one family, to another cable or component with a connector from a different family, which just cannot be done (without a crowbar). In steps the *adapter*. Adapters, which are sometimes referred to as coaxial adapters, are short, two-sided connectors with a connector from one family on one side and a connector from a different family on the other. Adapters facilitate connecting two RF "things" with connectors from different families. A variety of coaxial adapters is shown in Figure 5–12.

Figure 5–12 Coaxial adapters. *Courtesy of Amphenol.*

It requires three adapters (3 male-female combinations) to accommodate every *combination* of connector family. That means it takes 3 x 231, or 693 different adapters to accommodate all the different connector families shown in Table 5.5. Now you know why there are some RF companies that spend most of their time manufacturing adapters.

Waveguides

Another way RF signals get around is by something called *waveguides*. Waveguides are older technology, they are very expensive (compared to cables) and are used either for military or very high power applications. Waveguides are rarely used in today's commercial wireless systems—they are too darn big and they cost too much. Nevertheless, waveguides are still used. Several pieces of waveguide are shown in Figure 5–13.

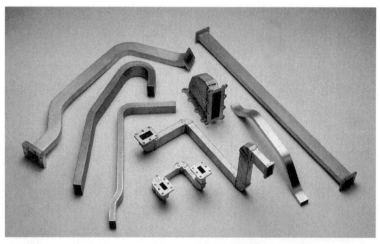

Figure 5–13 Waveguide. *Courtesy of A-Alpha Waveguide Co.*

Waveguides are essentially pipes, with a rectangular cross section, used to carry RF signals from one point to another. The interesting thing about waveguides is that, unlike cables which carry RF signals on a conductor, waveguides transport RF signals around as invisible waves. The waveguide merely serves to contain the waves and control their direction of travel.

If waveguides are old technology and they are large and expensive, why or where would they ever be used? What I forgot to mention about waveguides is that they have almost no insertion loss, which is why they are used in very high power RF systems. (And you thought there couldn't be a good reason.)

Circuit Traces

Hybrids and Printed Circuit Boards

The final way a signal can get around in an RF system is on a metal trace, mounted on top of some sort of dielectric material (remember dielectric?). If the dielectric happens to be ceramic and the components are all unpackaged "chips," then the circuit is a called a *hybrid* circuit or MIC (microwave integrated circuit). If the dielectric material happens to be some fancy plastic composite and the components are all packaged devices, then the circuit is called a *printed circuit*. A printed circuit is also referred to as a *printed circuit board* (PCB) and a discrete circuit. For examples of both, see Figures 5–4a and 5–4b in the section on Circuit Technologies.

Did You Know?

The fancy plastic composite materials used to make RF printed circuit boards are actually optimized to produce minimum insertion loss in the circuit (always a good thing). These plastic composites go by the names of FR4, PTFE, and Duroid™. Just thought you might like to know.

Stripline, Microstrip and Coplanar Waveguide

RF circuits can have their metal traces laid out several different ways. There are three ways which are particularly popular: *stripline*, *microstrip*, and *coplanar waveguide.*

Stripline tries to mimic a coaxial cable, only in circuit form. Coplanar waveguide tries to mimic a waveguide, only in circuit form, and microstrip doesn't try to mimic anything, it is just an RF circuit. All three layout schemes have their advantages and specific uses. Figure 5–14 shows a cross-sectional view of all three layout schemes. The dark areas are the metal traces and the light areas are the dialectic material.

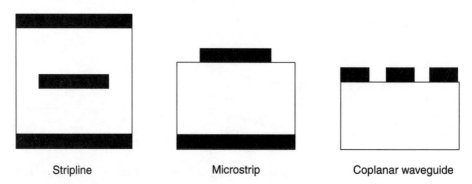

Stripline   Microstrip   Coplanar waveguide

Figure 5–14 Cross-sectional view of stripline, microstrip, and coplanar waveguide.

If you look closely at Figure 5–14, you can see that the cross section of stripline somewhat resembles the cross section of a coaxial cable (conductor in the middle, shield on the outside). And, if you look closely to the cross section of a coplanar waveguide (and you drink a fifth of whisky quickly), you still cannot see any resemblance to a real waveguide—because there isn't any. A coplanar waveguide may not look like a real waveguide, but it acts like it. Ask any RF engineer.

As a quick review, there are three ways which RF signals move around in an RF system: cables, waveguides, and metal traces on dielectric material. There are also two different types of RF circuits depending on the type of dielectric. If the dielectric is a ceramic, then the circuit is a hybrid (or a MIC). If the dielectric is a plastic composite, then the circuit is printed circuit (or PCB). There are three popular ways to lay out the circuit traces on RF circuits: stripline, microstrip, and coplanar waveguide. And finally, the goal of all the different media is the same: to move an RF signal from one point to another with the least amount of insertion loss.

Part 3

RF Systems

6

Older Technology

You might think with all the
current excitement about wire-
less communications that the technology has been
around for only a short time. Nothing could be further from
the truth, which is the topic of this chapter: wireless technologies which have
been around awhile. This chapter picks only three of these "older" technologies for discussion: broadcasting, radar, and satellite communication. But
even among these three there is a lot of variation in technology and system
design. These three were chosen as they represent a good cross section of the
various applications of RF technology.

AM radio, which has been around since the early 1920s, is an example
of broadcast technology, as are FM radio and television. Broadcast technology is a unique RF application in that it conveys information—wirelessly—
from one point to many points, with little concern for a response from the
intended receivers. Broadcasting is a one-way technology (which does not
keep people from screaming at their televisions). Recently, there has been
an assault on the broadcasters by those using a different wireless technology, namely, satellite service providers (also discussed in this chapter).

Radar technology, which has been around since the late 1930s, is an interesting form of RF communication. Unlike other forms of wireless communication, radar does not work by superimposing an information signal
onto an RF carrier (through modulation). Instead, the information is contained in slight changes in the RF carrier imposed on it by the environment.

As you will soon learn, these small changes can contain a lot of information about an object which the radar is following.

Today, radar is used almost everywhere: on the ground, in the air, and out in space. The availability of low cost RF electronics is enabling the use of radar technology in some surprising new places. The area experiencing the greatest impact from low-cost radar is the automobile industry. Some day in the not-so-distant future, all cars will come equipped with radar technology as a standard feature. (As far as I know, there is no plan to equip automobiles with missiles.)

Even satellite communication has been around since the early 1960s. It was first envisioned in the 1940s, but had to wait for technology to catch up to make it feasible. Satellites can be used for both one-way and two-way communications. If you have ever called someone in Hawaii (from outside the state), the call was routed by a satellite. And if you have ever watched a live sports event in a different time zone, that signal too was routed via satellite.

As you go through this chapter, you will see common themes among these three wireless technologies. You will notice that the Federal Communications Commission (FCC) in the United States and the International Telecommunications Union (ITU) everywhere else are responsible for allocating frequency for each application. You will see how each of these wireless applications can be described simply by a combination of a few of the basic RF building blocks discussed earlier in this book. This chapter also discusses the role that frequency plays in each system. In every case, the system is designed to use the latest technology to take full advantage of each particular system's frequency allocation.

The goal of this chapter is to help you understand, at a very basic level, the workings of wireless systems you are already familiar with. In each instance you are given an opportunity to "follow the signal" as it travels and to see what changes, if any, it undergoes during its journey. Once you understand the fundamental principals of these three technologies, you will have a general understanding of how all wireless systems work. Today's most sophisticated wireless technologies, like Doppler radar and low Earth orbit satellites, are merely refinements and improvements to these three basic systems.

BROADCASTING...

What is Broadcasting?

Characteristics

Broadcasting is nothing more than an RF system which transmits its signal over a "broad" geographic area and is intended for a "broad" audience. (You will never think of broadcasting the same way again.) Broadcasting is classified (in engineering speak) as a *one-to-many* system, which means there is one transmitter and many receivers. It also means there is no provision for the receiving party to communicate directly with the transmitting party. The three most recognizable broadcast applications are AM radio, FM radio, and television.

All forms of broadcasting in the United States have one thing in common: they have all been sanctioned, by the Federal Communications Commission (FCC), to operate within a very specific bandwidth. (Recall that a bandwidth is a frequency range uniquely defined by its upper and lower frequencies.) The FCC, being the kindhearted organization that it is, divides up these bandwidths into smaller bandwidths called *channels*, so that different broadcasters can transmit different things loosely referred to as entertainment.

Constraints

To comply with the FCC, broadcasters must operate within three constraints when transmitting their programs. Their first constraint is frequency. As mentioned above, each broadcaster is assigned a channel (frequency range) and can transmit RF energy only within that channel. Of course, to maintain order, everyone else is prohibited from broadcasting in that frequency range. Broadcasting is a perfect example of the need for filters in the output section of a transmitter.

The second constraint a broadcaster must obey is geography. Just because a radio station is granted the right to broadcast in San Francisco does not necessarily give it the right to broadcast in Oakland. In extreme cases, broadcasters have to "tailor" their radiated RF energy to conform to some agreed upon geographic boundary. If you recall from the discussion on antenna patterns, antennas can be designed to radiate RF energy in well-defined geometric patterns. Rarely, however, is there a need for such complex patterns (i.e., no clover leaves). A well positioned circle or oval will frequently do the trick.

Broadcasters place their transmitting antenna at the highest point in their allotted geographic region to ensure a "line of sight" to all the receivers. Suppose for a minute that the highest point (a hill) in a broadcaster's region happens to be at the northernmost point in the region. Further suppose that this northernmost point butts up against the southern edge of some other broadcaster's region (operating at the same frequency). In this situation, the first broadcaster is required to radiate RF energy strictly in the southerly direction (see Figure 6–1 for a visual depiction). By the way, it is entirely possible that the other region's broadcaster (broadcasting at the same frequency) will place their antenna on the same hill. They, of course, are required to transmit only in the northerly direction.

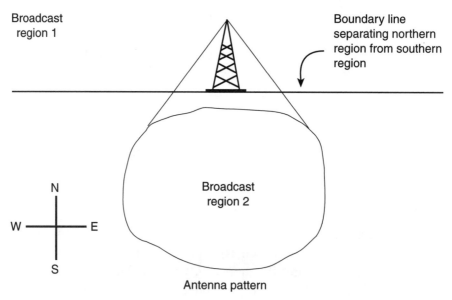

Figure 6–1   Antenna pattern of a broadcaster.

The final constraint a broadcaster must obey, closely related to geography, is power. There is a maximum limit to the amount of RF power a broadcaster can transmit. Two different RF behaviors serve to limit this power. First, as the transmitted power increases, the size of the antenna pattern grows (while the shape and direction stay the same). At some point, the antenna pattern will grow large enough to infringe on an adjacent broadcaster (operating at the same frequency). In Figure 6–1, if the antenna pattern grows too large, it will overlap the broadcast region to the south.

The other unwanted RF behavior, resulting from too much transmitted power, is due to the nature of the RF hardware. Because the output filter in a transmitter isn't perfect, as the RF power coming out of the transmitter within the broadcaster's allotted frequency range increases, so does the power coming out of the transmitter *outside* of the broadcaster's allotted frequency range. Above a certain power output, this power outside the allotted frequency range begins to interfere with channels in adjacent frequencies (operating in the same geographical region).

The Role of Frequency

Allocation

In the United States, the FCC has defined very specific frequency bands and channel allotments for AM radio, FM radio, and television (see Table 6–1).

Table 6–1   Broadcast Frequency Bands and Allotments

Service	Frequency Band(s)	Channel Allotment
AM radio	535–1605 kHz	10 kHz
FM radio	88–108 MHz	200 kHz
TV (VHF)	54–72 MHz	6 MHz
TV (VHF)	76–88 MHz	6 MHz
TV (VHF)	174–216 MHz	6 MHz
TV (UHF)	470–890 MHz	6 MHz

Your intuition should tell you that the greater the channel allotment (in frequency), the more information that can be broadcast, which is why AM radio, with its 10 kHz allotment, can only broadcast in mono, while FM radio, with its 200 kHz allotment, can broadcast in stereo, and TV, with its 6 MHz allotment, can broadcast video.

A quick look at the AM radio frequency allotment might lead you to the conclusion that, with a total frequency allocation of 1070 kHz (1605–535 kHz) and a channel allotment of 10 kHz, there will be 107 (1070 kHz ÷ 10 kHz) different channels in the AM band, which is not the case. In practice, radio channels are not mathematically adjacent to one another, but are separated by a small frequency "buffer" to ensure that consecutive channels do not interfere with each other.

Referring again to Table 6–1, the first TV frequency band (54–72 MHz) includes channels 2, 3, and 4. Since each channel is allocated 6 MHz and the total frequency range is only 18 MHz, it appears as though TV channels butt up against one another. In reality, each 6 MHz channel allotment contains a frequency buffer within it. You now have the ability to calculate the 6 MHz frequency allocation of any channel, since the channels are listed in order (by frequency) in Table 6–1. For instance, 76–82 MHz is channel 5, 82–88 MHz is channel 6, and so on. For those of you with too much free time, what frequency range corresponds to channel 51? (I should be mean and not tell you, but I won't.) It's 692–698 MHz, for whatever it's worth.

Did You Know?

You can probably figure out by now why high definition television (HDTV) has taken so long to become reality. All the television sets in the United States are designed to receive an entire program's information in only 6 MHz. HDTV signals contain more information than can be crammed into 6 MHz. (More bandwidth equals more information.) Of course, there is also the infighting among all of the various manufacturers over standards, but that's another story.

Propagation

The way a broadcast signal behaves in the environment has a lot to do with its frequency. Recall from an earlier chapter that when an RF signal, traveling in the air, encounters a solid object (e.g., a building), the signal either gets reflected or absorbed (or both). This behavior makes RF signals what is known as *line-of-sight* signals, which means that the transmitting antenna must be able to "see" the receiving antenna, without obstruction, for a wireless connection to be made.

Line-of-sight behavior has four implications for anyone trying to receive a television signal over the air. First, there must not be any major obstructions between the transmitting antenna and the television's antenna.

Second, the television's antenna must be constantly readjusted as all of the TV stations have their transmitting antennas located in different places. Third, trying to receive an over-the-air television signal in an area with tall buildings will probably result in a signal reception phenomenon called a *ghost*. A ghost is a double image in a TV's picture and it is very easy to understand. It is simply the result of a television receiving the same signal twice, at slightly different times. What causes a TV to receive the same signal twice? Signal reflections. One signal goes directly from the transmitting antenna to the television. The other signal reflects off of one or more large objects and then makes its way to the television. And since the second signal has farther to travel, it arrives later.

The final implication for line-of-sight signals, and probably the most significant for RF communications, is that to receive an RF signal the receiver must be within 25 miles of the (ground-based) transmitter or else the curvature of the Earth will make reception impossible. (Refer to Figure 6–7 to see a visual depiction of this.) There is one notable exception to this line-of-sight limitation, however. At lower frequencies (less than 30 MHz), signals can travel farther than line of sight by reflecting off the ionosphere (a layer of the Earth's atmosphere). This behavior explains why an AM radio station can occasionally be picked up at night from hundreds of miles away.

Tuning In

The Tuner

The following discussion pertains to television broadcasting, but it applies to AM and FM radio as well. Since all TV signals are only 6 MHz wide, the electronics within the television can only process signals between 0 and 6 MHz. This 6 MHz signal is what I have referred to as the "information" signal in earlier chapters. It contains all of the audio and video information necessary.

This presents a dilemma. The television's internal electronics can only accommodate signals between 0 and 6 MHz, but none of the transmitted signals are between 0 and 6 MHz. They are all at some higher frequency (see Table 6–1). How does the television get these higher frequency transmitted signals down to the frequency (called baseband) which the television's internal electronics can accommodate? It uses a device called a *tuner*. Before you start thinking that this tuner is some kind of a super-sophisticated piece of

RF electronics, realize it is nothing more than a variable filter followed by a mixer (see Figure 6–2).

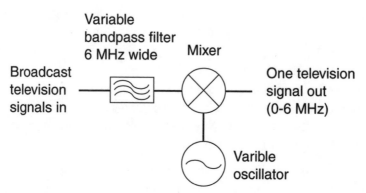

Figure 6–2   Block diagram of a TV tuner.

The tuner works in a two-step process. First, it selects the desired 6 MHz channel from all of the channels which are out there by adjusting the frequency of the variable bandpass filter to reject all of the unwanted signals, letting only the desired one pass. After which the mixer takes the one signal remaining and downconverts it to the baseband frequency (0–6 MHz). Note, that for the tuner to work properly, the oscillator needs to change its frequency for each different channel.

To help you visualize the workings of a tuner, refer to Figure 6–3. The upper graph is a frequency diagram showing all the channels which enter the tuner. After the variable filter, the only channel still remaining is the desired one, channel 51. (I figured you already knew the frequency band.) Of course, at this point the signal is at a frequency which is of no use to the television's electronics. After the mixer, however, channel 51 gets downconverted to baseband, where it is useful. It is at this point where the television's internal electronics take over, process the signal, and produce Seinfeld reruns.

Television Delivery

Three ways

There are basically three (legal) ways to receive a television signal today: over the air, by cable, or via satellite. While they use completely different methods to relay the signals, all three try to accomplish the same objective:

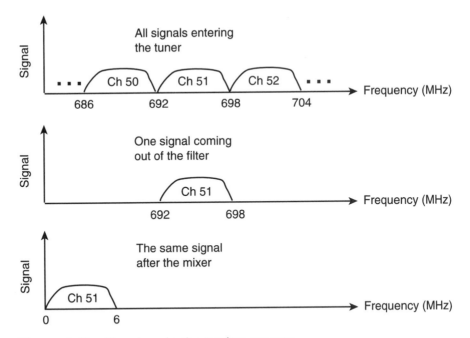

Figure 6–3 The steps in the tuning process.

to get as many different 6 MHz channels to your television set as possible. With over-the-air television, the number of 6 MHz channels is limited by the amount of *spectrum* (frequency bands) allocated by the FCC. This gives both cable and satellite a distinct advantage.

In the case of cable delivery, the cable itself carries signals between the frequencies of zero and approximately 1000 MHz. At 6 MHz per channel, this gives the cable the theoretical ability to carry 166 different channels. The reason it can transmit this many signals is because the signals are trapped within the cable and therefore do not interfere with over-the-air signals.

In the case of satellite TV, the satellite has the ability to deliver a tremendous number of television channels because of something called *digital signal processing*, which is covered in the section on satellites.

There is actually a fourth method of television delivery, which is a hybrid of the other three, called Multichannel Multipoint Distribution Service (MMDS). MMDS is covered in the section Fixed Wireless Applications in Chapter 7.

Cable TV providers do not deliver all 166 channels that they theoretically can. The reason they do not is because they have set aside a portion of the cable's frequency band (0–1000 MHz) for *RECEIVING* signals. Part of the cable's frequency band will be used for two-way communications, which makes it ideal for connecting to the Internet. Of course, since cable service was not originally intended for two-way communications, it may be some time before this service is available everywhere. Stay tuned.

Breaking News

I thought it might be interesting to show the path a television signal travels during a breaking news event—from the event to your TV. In this example, you will be exposed to all of the different roles which wireless communications play in an ordinary, everyday event.

Assume you are in your living room somewhere in Montana and you decide you need some entertainment and so you turn on the television. When you turn it on you discover that you are watching a high-speed police pursuit happening in Los Angeles (a daily occurrence). How has the signal reached your TV (refer to Figure 6–4)?

In this particular example, the news event is being filmed by a camera crew out in the field represented by the news van. The news van needs to get the live feed back to the local television station for processing and retransmission. The news van has the ability to transmit the signal wirelessly back to the TV station. Of course, it cannot send the signal directly back to the station because, more often than not, there are tall buildings and other obstructions interfering with the line of sight. (Remember line of sight?) So the news van sends the signal to the station indirectly, by way of a microwave relay tower (paths A and B in the figure) located at some high point in the city. This form of wireless communication is called point-to-point microwave communication, which is covered in the next chapter on fixed wireless communication.

After the signal reaches the local television station, the program manager decides that the news story is exciting enough even for people in Montana to see. So the local news station transmits the signal up to a satellite (path C), hovering over the United States, and the satellite in turn retransmits the signal back down to the local TV station in Montana (path D). (The satellite doesn't just retransmit the signal to Montana, it retransmits it to every place in the United States, but you will learn more about that in the forthcoming section on Satellite Communications.)

Finally, the local television station in Montana needs to get the signal to you, and since you live way out on a farm, you do not have cable TV. So the local station in Montana uses point-to-point microwave communication to get the signal to a high point in your area (path E). It is at this point where the signal becomes a "broadcast" signal for the first time and gets transmitted to you (path F), and all of your neighbors, of course. The signal you received used six different wireless paths and traveled over 45,000 miles just so you could laugh at some crazy person in Los Angeles. (Where would you be without wireless communications?)

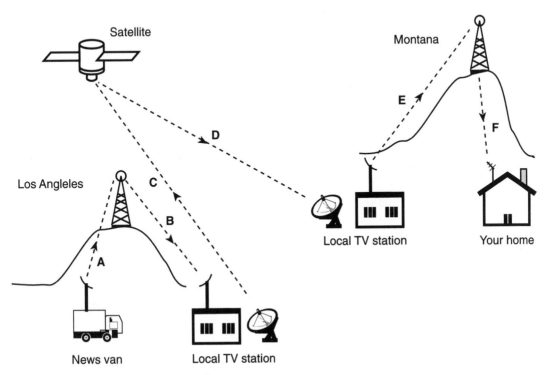

Figure 6–4   *The signal path of a news event.*

RADAR..

What is Radar?

Definition

Probably the most famous acronym in all of wireless communications, *radar* stands for RAdio Detecting And Ranging, which is a real big hint as to what it does. It uses radio waves to detect things. More specifically, today's advanced radars can measure four distinct characteristics about an object. Radar can detect if an object is present, how far away it is, where it is and, most impressively, how fast it is moving. (Anyone who has ever gotten a speeding ticket can attest to that.)

Radar is used in many places, including on the ground (called ground-based), on a ship (called shipboard), in the air (called airborne), and out in space (called spaced-based).

The Role of Frequency

Like every other wireless application in the United States, the FCC has allocated specific frequency bands for radar. Some of the allocated radar frequency bands are shown in Table 6–2.

Table 6–2 Some Radar Frequency Bands

Radar Band	Frequency Range(s)	Some Uses
UHF	220–225 MHz	Early warning, satellite surveillance.
VHF	420–450 MHz	Early warning, satellite surveillance.
L-band	960–1215 MHz	Air traffic control.
S-band	2.3–2.5 GHz 2.7–3.0 GHz	Shipboard military, early warning.
C-band	5.25 -5.925 GHz	Altimeters, weather.

Table 6–2   Some Radar Frequency Bands (Continued)

Radar Band	Frequency Range(s)	Some Uses
X-band	8.5–10.55 GHz	Airborne fighter, weather, police.
Ku-band	13.4–14 GHz 15.7–17.7 GHz	Airborne fighter, police.

There are four main factors which dictate what frequency is selected for a particular application. All four, which are highlighted in Table 6–3, must be taken into account when making the frequency decision. Notice in Table 6–3 that several of the words are surrounded by quotes, which is because each of these is a relative measure. For instance, a "large" radar system for airborne applications will probably be considered a "small" radar system for ground-based applications.

Table 6–3   Factors Affecting Frequency Selection in Radar Systems

Factors	Implication
As the frequency goes up, the atmospheric absorption (attenuation) goes up.	If the radar needs to detect something "far" away, a "low" frequency is required.
As the frequency goes up, the size of the system's components gets smaller.	If space is limited (as on an airplane), the frequency must be "high."
For a given frequency, as the antenna size gets bigger, the beamwidth gets smaller.	If radar accuracy is important, a "large" antenna is needed.
As the output power goes up, the system size and weight goes up.	If "high" power is required, a "large" space is needed to house the radar.

Table 6–3 contains a word you may not have seen before called *beamwidth*. The beamwidth of a radiated RF signal describes how wide the antenna pattern is from an antenna which is *not* omnidirectional. (See Figure 3–6 for a review of antenna patterns.) As you recall, an antenna which is not omnidirectional radiates RF energy in only one specific direction. Of course, RF energy can be radiated in a wide pattern or a narrow pattern (see Figure 6–

5). Antenna beamwidths are measured in degrees (of a circle). With respect to the antenna patterns in Figure 6–5, the antenna on the left has a narrow beamwidth (perhaps 10 degrees out of 360) while the antenna on the right has a wide beamwidth (perhaps 45 degrees out of 360).

It should be intuitive that the narrower the beamwidth, the more accurately a radar's antenna can locate an object. As with all aspects of the RF world, there is a price to be paid for this accuracy. As mentioned in Table 6–3, a narrow beamwidth (i.e., more accuracy) requires a large antenna, which is heavy and difficult to move.

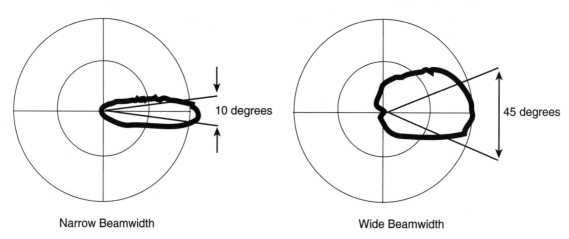

Narrow Beamwidth   Wide Beamwidth

Figure 6–5   A comparison of antenna beamwidths.

How Radar Works

The Role of Reflection

Radar works off the simple principal, covered back in Chapter 2, that when an RF signal encounters a solid object, at least some of the RF energy is reflected. The key concept to this RF "reflection" is something called *radar cross section*. Every solid object has a radar cross section. Radar cross section can be visualized by viewing the two-dimensional silhouette of any three-dimensional object. To help you envision this, imagine looking at a football straight on at the pointy end. Even though the football is oblong and comes to a point, when viewed from its end the radar cross section of a football is a perfect circle. It's like looking at a football which has been cut in half.

The fundamental principal of radar is this: the greater the area of the cross section, the more RF energy which gets reflected, and the more RF energy which gets reflected, the easier it is to find the object. Remember, it isn't the size of the object which matters, but the area of its radar cross section (silhouette). In that respect, a football is easier for radar to find than a fishing rod.

Did You Know?

The B-2 bomber in the United States Air Force is almost invisible to radar. It accomplishes this feat in two ways. First, the entire outside of the plane is covered with an RF absorbing material. Almost all of the RF energy (radar from an enemy) that hits the plane gets absorbed (converted to heat) rather than reflected. Second, the unique design of the plane gives it an incredibly small radar cross section when viewed from the front. It's almost like looking at a pencil, which also has a small radar cross section.

How Radar Determines Distance

To determine an object's distance—and consequently its presence—the radar simply invokes the easiest equation you ever learned back in Algebra: distance equals rate times time (D = R x T). The key to using this equation is that the radar system already knows the rate (at which the RF signal is traveling). RF waves travel at the speed of light, which just happens to be 186,000 miles per second. To put it in perspective, light can race around the equator of the Earth almost eight times in one second. (And you thought Ferraris were fast.)

In determining distance, the radar's transmitter sends out a signal and the super-fast electronics within the radar counts the time until the reflected signal reaches the receiver. Dividing this count by two (because the RF energy has to travel there and back), gives the time required for the signal to reach the object. This time, multiplied by the speed of light, determines the distance to the object. Radar systems which only determine distance are known as pulsed radars, because it "pulses" the transmitter off and on. During its brief "on" period, the transmitter sends out RF energy at a particular frequency. During its off period, the receiver "listens" for the reflected signal. Since the reflected signal is at the same frequency as the original (transmitted) signal, the transmitter must be off while the receiver listens for the reflected signal. (Otherwise, all the receiver hears is the transmitted signal.)

Did You Know?

Back in the 17th century, Sir Isaac Newton—the genius that discovered gravity—actually tried to measure the speed of light. He did so by standing on top of a mountain with a lantern and he had a colleague stand on another mountain, not far away, with another lantern. Newton's intention was to uncover his lantern and, upon seeing the light, have his partner uncover his lantern. All Newton needed to do was to count the time between uncovering his own lantern and seeing the other light, divide by two and he had the speed of light, or so he thought. Needless to say, this did not work very well, given the infinitesimal time it took for the light to make the trip. However, rumor has it that it did cause Newton to ponder his dilemma by sitting under an apple tree.

How Radar Determines Direction

Radar determines an object's location by moving the antenna in a process called *scanning*. Scanning involves pointing the antenna in a single direction, transmitting a signal in that direction, and waiting for the reflected signal. If a reflected signal is received, the radar knows which way the antenna is pointing and therefore it knows in what direction the object is located.

After a short period of time, the antenna moves a small amount and repeats the process. The radar repeats this three step process (move antenna, transmit a signal, wait for a reflection) until it has covered the entire area of interest and then points the antenna back to the first position and starts the process all over again.

This is where beamwidth size comes in. Smaller beamwidths require more of these "antenna moves" in the scanning process but allow the radar to pinpoint the object more exactly. Obviously there is a trade-off. Narrower beamwidths take longer to find the object, but once it's found its location is known more precisely. When airborne radar is used in combat, a wide beamwidth is initially used to scan, just to know if there is something out there. Once an object is detected, a narrower beamwidth is used to pinpoint the actual location of the target.

Think about all of the different trade-offs which need to be made in designing a radar system. If you are the pilot of a fighter aircraft and you are hunting down enemy aircraft, you want a radar which can produce a very narrow beamwidth so that you can locate the target precisely before you fire your missile. A narrow beamwidth requires one of two things: either a big antenna or a high frequency of transmission. A big antenna is an excellent choice if it does not keep the aircraft from taking off in the first place. Obviously, there is a limitation. On the other hand, a high frequency is a good choice to produce a narrow beamwidth, except for one thing: high frequencies suffer from extreme atmospheric attenuation, which means that the radar can only locate the closest of targets. If I were flying a fighter aircraft, I'd want to see *all* of the targets (near and far). Today's radars are a combination of constant technological innovation and performance tradeoffs.

Did You Know?

One of the drawbacks to conventional radar is that it requires the antenna to physically move to scan the area of interest. Not only does it require expensive motors to move the (heavy) antenna, but it is impossible for the antenna to move from one position to another, non-adjacent position instantaneously. As a result of this limitation, a new technology has been developed called electronically scanned arrays, in which the antenna pattern in the radar moves without anything physically moving. To understand the details of this would truly require a degree in engineering, so you will just have to take my word for it.

How Radar Determines Velocity

Back in the 1800s, a clever Austrian physicist named Christian Doppler made an amazing discovery. He observed that the frequency of sound waves emanating from a moving object changed as the object moved by. And as things turned out, it isn't just true for sound waves but all waves including RF. In fact, this observed "frequency shift" (called a Doppler shift) is proportional to the velocity of the moving object. This is the fundamental principal underlying what is known as *Doppler radar*. Doppler radar is used to determine an object's velocity. It is Doppler radar which is responsible for all the "false" readings the police use to give out speeding tickets.

Doppler radar is somewhat different from conventional radar in that the transmitter is always on. This type of radar is known as *continuous wave* or CW radar. The transmitter must stay on continuously because, unlike conventional radar which counts the time between transmission and reception, Doppler radar is looking for a change in frequency. Since this change in frequency may not last long, the transmitter must stay on continuously.

You may be wondering why the transmitter doesn't interfere with the receiver if it is always on? It would, if the receiver were listening for the same frequency which the transmitter is transmitting, but it isn't. It is looking for a signal which is frequency *shifted* from the transmitted signal. In fact, the receiver filters out any reflected signals at the transmitter's frequency. Reflected signals at the transmitter's frequency are, by definition, not moving (there is no frequency shift). Doppler radar does not care about stationary objects.

Perhaps you are thinking that in certain circumstances it would be advantageous to combine the capabilities of conventional radar (distance and location) with the capability of Doppler radar (velocity). In fact, today's most sophisticated radar systems, called pulsed Doppler radar, do just that. It not only counts the time lapse of the received signal (to determine distance), but it also looks for frequency shifts (to determine velocity).

Did You Know?

If you have ever heard a train whistle's tone change as it passed by you, you have experienced a Doppler shift. What you heard, as the train came toward you, was the frequency of the train's whistle "shifted" by the velocity of the train. Since the train was coming toward you, the frequency was shifted up. As the train passed by you, the tone dropped, shifted downward by the velocity of the train going away from you.

Different Radar Systems

Pulsed Radar Systems

As mentioned before, pulsed radar systems are used to calculate distance and, as a consequence, presence. Two common systems using pulsed radar are automatic door openers (found at many supermarkets) and automatic toilet flushers (found in many airports). The systems' operations are simple to understand. In both cases the system continuously transmits a radar pulse and waits for a response. The systems expect to receive a response at one of two time intervals. In the case when no person is present, the signal reflects off of the ground (for the door opener) or off the lavatory door (for the flusher), which result in a "long" time delay. With this long time delay, the system knows to do nothing. When a person is present, the signal in both cases reflects off of the person, which is closer to the system, resulting in a shorter time interval. When the system senses this shorter time interval, it knows to do its thing (open the door or flush the toilet).

A new application for pulsed radar is called *near object detection system* or NODS. NODS is nothing more than an inexpensive pulsed radar on the rear bumper of an automobile. When the car is put in reverse, the radar turns on and begins pulsing and timing the response. While backing up, if the car gets too close to an object (the time delay gets too short), it signals a warning—which should make parallel parking easier.

Did you ever wonder how commercial airline pilots know what altitude the airplane is at? They know because they use a clever little device called an *altimeter.* You have probably heard the word before but did not know what it was or how it worked. Well, now you do. An altimeter is nothing more than pulsed radar in an airplane, pointing down at the ground. It sends out a signal, waits for a response, and converts the time delay into a distance (see Figure 6–6), which is the airplane's altitude.

Now for the fun part. If an airplane is cruising at 33,000 feet, how long does it take for the round trip of the altimeter's signal? That is 66,000 feet (the length of the signal's round trip) divided by 984 million feet per second (the speed of light), or about 67 millionths of a second. (I guess that's what they mean by how time flies.)

Another useful pulsed radar system is weather radar. It works simply by detecting the RF energy reflected off of raindrops. No rain, no reflection; a little rain, a little reflection; a lot of rain, a lot of reflection. These differences in reflected RF power show up as different colors on the weather maps shown on the evening news. And, of course, taking several of these (radar) weather readings periodically results in the "moving cloud" display which captures everyone's attention during hurricane season.

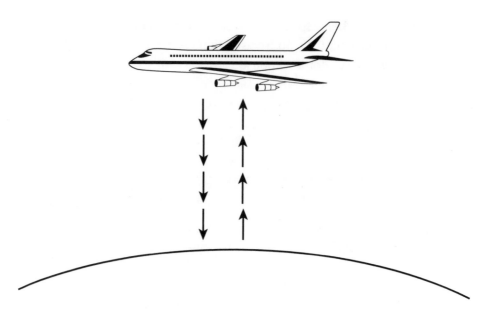

Figure 6–6   *The signal path of a radar altimeter.*

Doppler Radar Systems

The most common use of Doppler radar is the radar gun used by your local law enforcement to punish you for running late. The radar gun simply detects the change in frequency from the signal reflected off the automobile and converts it to a speed in miles per hour. (I understand that the next generation of radar guns will be able to convert a car's speed measurement directly into a debit in a checking account.)

A more interesting use of Doppler radar, used in fighter aircraft, is called *fire control radar*. (It is called fire control radar because it "controls" the "firing" of the aircraft's missiles.) In today's modern aircraft, pulsed Doppler radar is used to determine both location and velocity.

In the nose of every fighter aircraft is a pulsed Doppler radar. In air combat, fighter pilots only care about situations (called threats) in which an enemy aircraft is coming toward them. The pulsed Doppler radar uses a wide beamwidth in the pulsed mode to scan (remember scanning?) the sky for any threats. Once it detects a threat, the radar locks onto the target with a narrow beam. The receiver then analyzes the return signal for one of three conditions: no change in frequency, a lower frequency, or a higher frequency.

When the receiver senses no change in frequency, it is implied that there is no relative difference in the velocities of the two airplanes, which means the enemy plane is traveling away from the pilot's plane at exactly the same speed. Interpretation: the enemy pilot is prudent.

When the receiver senses a drop in frequency, it means that the enemy plane is traveling away at a greater velocity and thereby increasing the distance from the pilot's plane. Interpretation: the enemy pilot is chicken. Finally, if the receiver senses an increase in frequency, it means that the enemy aircraft is heading right for the pilot, and the greater the frequency shift, the faster the enemy is closing in. Interpretation: the enemy pilot is crazy.

Did You Know?

Police radar jammers—which may be illegal—work by transmitting an RF signal at a constantly varying frequency within the frequency band of the radar gun. The radar gun is expecting to receive a single frequency (which reflects the speed of the car). Instead, it receives a whole bunch of different frequencies which drives the display crazy. Oh well.

The police aren't the only ones having fun with Doppler radar. Weather forecasters are also taking advantage of it. Believe it or not, Doppler radar can be made to measure the velocity of wind. How it does this depends on the RF energy's ability to reflect off moving air differently than static air. With this capability, Doppler radar is used to detect things such as wind shear, which is a strong and sudden change in the wind's direction near the ground (usually near airports).

The last radar I will mention, only briefly, is a relatively new system called *collision avoidance*. Collision avoidance is similar to NODS, only for the front of an automobile. It has the ability to detect distance and velocity of objects in front of the car. With both of these pieces of information, an on-board computer determines whether the car in front is too close for the speed it is traveling. If the car is too close, the system either gently applies the brakes or berates the driver incessantly about their overly aggressive driving behavior.

The reason that you may not have seen collision avoidance systems on automobiles yet (circa 1999) is that car manufacturers in the U.S., Europe and Asia cannot agree on which frequency band to use. Stay tuned.

SATELLITE COMMUNICATIONS ....

Why Satellites?

Satellite technology evolved from a limitation of RF behavior: line-of-sight transmission. If the earth were flat, this line-of-sight behavior would not be an issue (which is *one* of the reasons there were no satellites before Columbus.) A signal transmitted in any direction which has sufficient power will get to its intended receiver, and over (relatively) short distances, this is exactly what happens. The problem arises when an RF signal is transmitted over long distances (greater than 25 miles) and the receiver is obscured by the curvature of the Earth (see Figure 6–7).

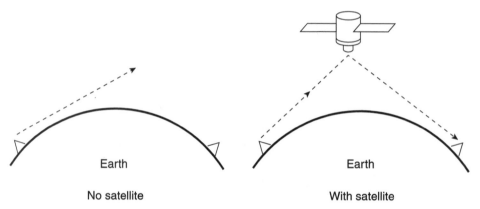

	Earth		Earth
No satellite		With satellite	

Figure 6–7   *Line-of-sight behavior and the satellite solution.*

The left side of Figure 6–7 demonstrates what happens to RF signals which have sufficient power to travel over 25 miles. They head toward outer space. This behavior, while a limitation, is also a benefit. Because of this behavior, the FCC can allocate the same frequency to different parties in different geographical locations. After about 25 miles, the signal is no longer Earthbound and it therefore no longer interferes with other signals which are at the same frequency.

An interesting thing to note is that there is an exception to the behavior depicted on the left side of Figure 6–7. As previously mentioned in the section on broadcasting, at low RF frequencies (less than 30 MHz), the RF energy gets reflected off the ionosphere and "bent" around the earth. Satellites are not needed for signals at these frequencies.

Arthur C. Clarke, who wrote *2001: A Space Odyssey*, among other things, actually conceived of the idea of communication satellites back in 1945. This is a pretty insightful observation, given the fact that space travel did not even exist yet. Maybe he got the idea from his buddy, Hal.

The right side of Figure 6–7 shows all you need to know about the utility of satellites. Satellites allow RF signals to overcome the curvature of the Earth and still obey their line-of-sight behavior.

Given the tremendous expense involved in launching and maintaining satellites, they are only used for long distance communications. You will probably never see people using satellite communications to call their next door neighbor.

How Satellites Work

Geosynchronous Orbit

The satellite systems used for intercontinental telecommunications and television re-transmission work for only one reason: the satellite does not move with respect to the Earth. This is a pretty good trick since the Earth is rotating at about 1000 miles per hour at the equator.

It just so happens that there is one specific orbit around the Earth, located 22,000 miles up from the equator, called *geosynchronous orbit* (GEO). (It is also referred to as *geostationary orbit*.) It is in this orbit where a satellite can rotate around the Earth at the same rotational speed as the Earth. A satellite rotating around the Earth in geosynchronous orbit appears to remain stationary when viewed from a point on the equator. (If the satellite did not remain fixed, the direction of the transmitted signal from the ground would have to be continually altered.)

How does geosynchronous orbit work? Without going back to Physics 101, there are two forces pulling the satellite in different directions, and at the GEO these two forces cancel each other out. One of these forces is the centrifugal force. You can envision centrifugal force by picturing yourself whipping a ball on a string around your head. If you let go, the ball goes flying outward. The other force acting on the satellite is gravity, which tries to pull the satellite inward (toward Earth). At 22,000 miles above the equator, these two forces cancel each other out and the satellite does not move with respect to the Earth.

As a visual appreciation for how high up 22,000 miles is, Figure 6.8 is an approximate scale of the Earth and the satellite's distance above it. Because the satellite is so high above the Earth, it is a good news/bad news situation. The bad news is that because the satellite is so high up, it takes a lot of RF power to reach it from the Earth. The good news is that signals transmitted down from the satellite can reach almost an entire hemisphere. Therefore, a satellite used to forward telephone calls from the United States to Great Britain is located halfway across the Atlantic Ocean, at the equator, of course.

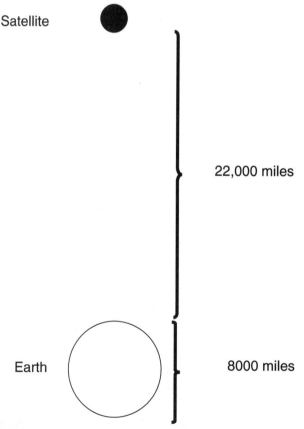

Figure 6–8   *The relative height of a GEO satellite.*

When a GEO satellite is launched from onboard the space shuttle, it is only about 300 miles up when it is jettisoned from the craft. It still has another 21,700 miles to go before it reaches GEO. Why bother launching from the shuttle, you ask? It just so happens that the first 300 miles is where all the gravity is, not to mention that is where all the rockets blow up.

Uplink/Downlink

Once the satellite is comfortably situated in GEO, the next areas of concern are the *uplink* and the *downlink*. The uplink describes the signal which travels from the ground transmitter (called the *Earth station*) up to the satellite receiver, while the downlink describes the signal which travels from the satellite transmitter to the ground receiver.

The uplink and downlink frequency bands for satellite systems are allocated by the FCC in the United States (just like every other form of RF communication). Since some satellites are used for international communications, the downlink frequencies impact countries other than the United States. The responsibility for allocating these "international" frequencies falls on the International Telecommunications Union (ITU). Think of the ITU as the FCC for the rest of the world.

A really ingenious feature of satellite communications is that the uplink frequency band and the downlink frequency band (in a given system) are never the same. When signals traveling in different directions use different frequency bands, it is called *duplex* communications. A satellite used for telecommunications is an example of duplex communication. The implication of duplex communication is that when you can call somebody in another country, halfway around the world, using satellite communications, both of you can speak at the same time. (This advantage is somewhat diminished if you don't speak the other person's language.)

However, when talking to someone using satellite communications there is another issue to be considered called *propagation delay*. Recall how RF energy travels at the speed of light. The time it takes a signal to travel across town, using a cellular phone, is inconsequential and cannot be detected by human beings (or any other beings). Satellite communication is different. With a round trip of 44,000 miles, there is a one-quarter-second delay between the originating transmitter and the ending receiver. Of course, this delay is only in one direction. When trying to hold a conversation in which the other person also gets to speak, the round trip delay is half of one second. (Two round trips are made to the satellite.) This one half second delay is very noticeable when making an intercontinental telephone call.

The one-quarter-second delay is also present when viewing a sports event from another continent. Of course, in the case of broadcasting, the one-quarter-second delay is of little consequence, unless finding out the result of the World Cup final 250 milliseconds after the people in the stadium bothers you.

Satellite Dishes

Earth stations transmit and receive signals with dish antennas (see Figure 6–9) because they are highly directional (they have a narrow beamwidth). The size of the dish antenna used depends on the frequency and power of the uplink and downlink signals. High uplink power requires a large dish. On the other hand, high downlink power only requires a small dish (like that used for direct-to-home TV).

When receiving the downlink signal, dish antennas act as funnel reflectors. First, they funnel as much of the RF energy (from the satellite) as possible into the dish, which is made of an RF reflecting material. Obviously, the bigger the dish, the more RF energy it can funnel, which is why high power satellites, like the ones used in direct-to-home TV, only require a small dish. Once the RF energy enters the dish, it all gets reflected to a single "focal" point, slightly elevated from the surface of the dish (see Figure 6–9). This focal point contains the actual antenna element and the low noise amplifier (LNA).

Footprints

The antenna on a satellite projects an antenna pattern just like every other antenna. (Recall from Chapter 3 how an antenna pattern is a visual display of the direction which RF energy is radiating out from an antenna.) Because the antenna pattern generated from a satellite is projected onto the surface of the Earth, it is called an antenna *footprint*. The power radiated inside this footprint is called the *effective isotropic radiated power*, or EIRP. (I guess just plain "radiated power" was already taken.) A graphical depiction of an antenna footprint covering the United States is shown in Figure 6–10.

Figure 6–9 A satellite dish antenna. *Courtesy of Andrew Corp.*

    Notice from Figure 6–10 that the antenna pattern approximately covers
the land area of the continental United States. This is not by accident. There
is only a finite amount of RF energy being transmitted from the satellite, and
while the satellite is high enough in GEO to transmit a signal which covers
half the globe, why bother. (Other than television-watching whales, who
would know the difference?) Covering half the globe results in less power
reaching the United States. This leads to an interesting aspect of satellite
footprints. They can be contoured, somewhat, to approximate the shape of
the area they are designed to cover to make maximum use of the available RF
power.

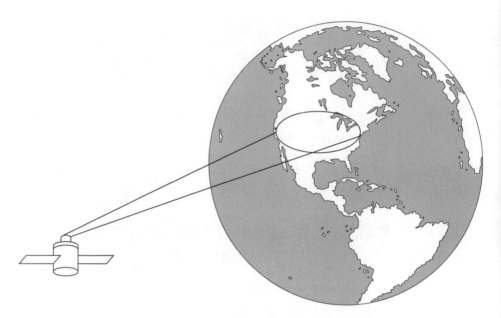

Figure 6–10 *A satellite footprint covering the United States.*

Satellite footprints are predominantly in the shape of a circle or oval. With respect to Figure 6–10, it might appear that certain parts of the United States receive no signal at all (those outside the footprint), which is not the case. Recall that an antenna pattern is a silhouette of an area which receives some minimum amount of RF energy. In this figure, the area outside of the oval still receives RF energy; it's just less than the area inside. There are some ramifications to a footprint not covering the entire United States. Under certain adverse conditions (e.g., heavy rain), it is entirely possible that those areas which lie outside the footprint will receive a degraded (or no) signal.

The footprint shown in Figure 6–10 is for a broadcast signal. It is obviously meant to be received by many different points in the United States. More than likely this is some kind of television broadcast. But what if the satellite carries intercontinental telephone calls; what will the footprint look like then? It will still be a circle or oval, only much smaller and focused only on the long distance telephone carrier's Earth station.

RF Electronics

By now you are probably wondering what the RF electronics on board a satellite consists of. (Even if you're not, that's what you're about to read.) At its most basic, the RF electronics on board a satellite, called a *transponder*, is just a simple combination of a few RF devices (see Figure 6–11).

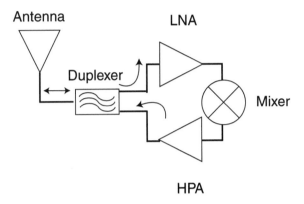

Figure 6–11 Block diagram of a satellite transponder.

Referring to Figure 6–11, the satellite antenna receives the uplink signal (at the uplink frequency) and sends it on to the duplexer. (Recall that a duplexer is nothing more than two bandpass filters in one box.) The duplexer then routes the signal to the low noise amplifier (LNA), which amplifies the signal. Next, the mixer frequency shifts the signal to the downlink frequency (source not shown) and, finally, the signal gets boosted by the high power amplifier (HPA) and sent through the duplexer on its way out the antenna. Figure 6–11 is a block diagram which describes the basic RF function of every satellite which has ever had the good fortune to make it all the way to GEO.

About the Spacecraft

GEO satellites do not last forever, but it is not because the RF electronics fail. (If nothing else, RF engineers build reliable satellites.) In fact, the RF electronics on board a satellite can last almost indefinitely, and because it gets its power from the sun (via solar panels), there should be no reason why a satellite does not last forever. Except for one thing. For GEO satellites to work properly, they need to stay fixed in GEO and, unfortunately, over time, satellites tend to drift a little. (Ok, so GEO isn't perfect.) To counteract this natural tendency to drift, satellites are equipped with something called *station-keeping*.

Station-keeping is nothing more than an onboard propulsion system which periodically releases small bursts of fuel. The momentum shift from these small bursts serves to reposition the satellite in its proper place. A satellite only carries a limited amount of this fuel, so when it runs out, the satellite can no longer be repositioned and quickly becomes useless. Just prior to using up the last of the fuel, the onboard propulsion system gives one big burst and sends the satellite to a different, out-of-the-way orbit, where it spends the remainder of its existence in the lonely, dark void of space.

Satellite Systems

Three Topologies

There are three basic topologies used in satellite communications: point-to-point, point-to-multipoint, and multipoint-to-point. Which topology is used is dictated by the application.

One example of point-to-point topology is intercontinental telecommunications. When a bunch of people in Great Britain want to call a bunch of people in the United States, their calls first go to an Earth station in Great Britain. All of the calls are combined into one signal and transmitted to a telecommunications satellite hanging out somewhere over the Atlantic Ocean (at the equator, of course). The signal is then retransmitted (by the satellite) to an Earth station in the United States (owned by one of the long distance carriers). The calls are then separated and routed along their way to their final destinations. In this example, the satellite is used to connect a single point (the Earth station in Great Britain) to a single point (the Earth station in the United States). In point-to-point topology, only two large satellite dishes are required and both are used to transmit and receive.

Point-to-multipoint topology is used in direct-to-home satellite television (called DBS for *direct broadcast satellite*). For broadcasts in the United States, a single Earth station, owned by the broadcast company, transmits its "entertainment" up to a satellite (situated somewhere over Kansas). The satellite then retransmits the signal in a footprint which covers the whole country, like the one shown in Figure 6–10. Anybody with a small dish antenna, located within (or near) the footprint, will be able to—for $29.99/month—receive the broadcast signal. In point-to-multipoint topology, there is one large dish for transmitting and many small dishes for receiving (only).

The most frequent use of multipoint-to-point topology is something called VSAT, which stands for *very small aperture terminal*. In this topology, many Earth stations with small to medium size dishes are used to relay information from a point of sale back to a single location, typically the central office. One of the big users of VSATs are gasoline companies. Quite often you will see gasoline stations with small satellite dishes on their roofs. This is a VSAT system. The system periodically relays sales information from the station, via satellite, back to the main office. In this way, the main office has an up-to-the-minute status on the sale of gasoline all over the country. In multipoint-to-point topology, there are many small dishes transmitting and only one dish receiving.

The Role of Frequency

The FCC has allocated many different frequency bands for what it calls Fixed Satellite Service, which is the government's way of saying GEO. By far, the two most popular frequency bands used for commercial Fixed Satellite Service are C-band and Ku-band. The specifics of C-band and Ku-band are shown in Figure 6–4.

Table 6–4   C-Band and Ku-Band Frequency Allocations

Band	Frequency Allocation
C-band downlink	3.7–4.2 GHz
C-band uplink	5.925–6.425 GHz
Ku-band downlink	11.7–12.2 GHz
Ku-band uplink	14.0–14.5 GHz

Wherever there is a home outfitted with a large dish antenna, it is probably receiving a C-band downlink (originally intended just for reception by the broadcast stations). If they have a small dish antenna, chances are it is Ku-band (direct-to-home satellite TV).

For a given satellite system, the uplink signal is always at a higher frequency than the downlink signal. Do you know why? It is because RF electronics are less efficient at higher frequencies, which translates to more wasted power. Now where do you suppose RF engineers would rather locate the more wasteful electronics—on the ground, where power is plentiful, or in space, where power is at a premium? Take your time.

If you recall, the RF section of a satellite, called a transponder, is used to frequency shift the uplink signal to the frequency of the downlink signal. In today's satellites, there is more than one transponder in a given frequency band. For instance, C-band, with a downlink bandwidth of 500 MHz (3.7 GHz–4.2 GHz) has 12 transponders to cover the entire bandwidth. The 500 MHz bandwidth is divided into 12, equally sized bandwidths (42 MHz each) called *channels*. Each transponder is assigned a channel. There are many reasons for breaking up the total bandwidth into channels, but by far the most important is redundancy. If there are 12 transponders and one fails, there are still 11 left, but if there is only one transponder and it fails, you get the picture. (Besides, do you have any idea how hard it is to get an RF technician into GEO?)

The main goal of every satellite user is to make maximum use of the available bandwidth on the satellite. Transponder bandwidth, called *capacity*, is leased out at a very expensive hourly rate. Satellite users try to cram as much information as possible into every MHz of every transponder. Take the case of standard broadcast television. Recall from earlier in this chapter when I mentioned that a standard broadcast television signal requires 6 MHz of bandwidth. But transponders have 42 MHz of bandwidth. What do you suppose the TV stations do? If you guessed that they cram seven different channels into each transponder, you're on the right track, but you forgot about polarization. (You are forgiven if you didn't read that section.) Polarization allows TV broadcasters to cram 14 (7 horizontally polarized and 7 vertically polarized) different television channels into one transponder.

In more sophisticated satellite systems today, the 6 MHz television signal is digitized before it is transmitted up to the satellite. Why digitize it? Once a signal is digitized, it can be compressed in a process called *digital compression* (what else?) with the use of digital signal processors (DSP). Digital compression involves removing redundant information in the TV signal, resulting in less bandwidth required to transmit the signal. After compression, a 6 MHz signal may only take up 4 MHz, and you know what that means: more television channels into the same transponder (and more money into the satellite owner's pocket).

Did You Know?

(Digital) data compression is very simple to understand. Picture a 50-page book in which every page has the same exact words, "good morning." (A pretty boring book, I admit.) For you to know exactly what is in the book, you could read all 50 pages. Or, I could compress the book by writing on the first page, "good morning, the next 50 pages say the same exact thing." Now you can read one page and know what all 50 pages say, because I got rid of the redundant information. That is data compression.

To give you an appreciation for the capacity of a 42 MHz transponder channel, an (uncompressed) telephone call requires 4 kHz of bandwidth, which means each transponder channel can carry over 10,000 different voice calls simultaneously (ignoring polarization).

A Special Satellite System—GPS

What is GPS?

GPS, or *global positioning system*, is a satellite system consisting of 21 satellites which do nothing but continuously transmit a strange, but useful, signal. GPS satellites offer no provision for receiving signals from their users. The signals transmitted from the GPS satellites are used for two things: navigation and timing. The signals allows anyone with a GPS receiver to know approximately where they are on the surface of the Earth. (I say approximately because there is always some error in the measurement, which ranges from inches to miles, depending on many things.) The GPS signals can also be used to tell what time it is, but then again so can a wristwatch.

When a GPS receiver is used to determine present location, it does not respond with something like "the corner of 5th and Market in downtown Pittsburgh." Instead, what it gives is a measurement in degrees of longitude and latitude, and while knowing your present location by longitude and latitude is interesting, by itself it isn't particularly useful (unless you happen to be Gilligan). Conveniently, today's GPS receivers come with a trip function, which enables it to remember your starting point and give you relative distance and direction measurements from that point, as you travel. For instance, if you are hiking in a densely wooded area which you are unfamiliar with, at your launching point you can command the GPS receiver to store that location in memory. Then, at any point in the trip, if you ask the GPS receiver how to get back, it will relay how far and in what direction you need to go to get there. Now that is useful.

An interesting thing about the GPS satellites is that they are *not* in geosynchronous orbit, which means they are not stationary, with respect to the rotation of the Earth. If you could see them from Earth (you would be Superman), you would see GPS satellites cruising by overhead periodically from one horizon to the other. Since each of the 21 satellites more or less transmits the same signal, and since there is no need for them to *receive* any signals, as long as some of the satellites are overhead at any moment in time—even though they are moving—the system works just fine.

Did You Know?

The GPS satellite system, deployed by the Department of Defense, was originally intended solely for the purpose of enabling soldiers in the battlefield to know their exact position. Of course, today it has many more uses. One of the most exciting is a service called E911, in which a cellular phone is equipped with a GPS receiver. In the event you break down, not only can you use your cellular phone to call for help, but the GPS receiver relays your location to the emergency service so they know where to find you.

Theory of Operation

GPS operates on the same basic principal as radar: if the time it takes for a signal to reach a certain point is known, then its distance can also be calculated. A GPS receiver receives specially encoded signals from the GPS satellites which enables it to determine how long it took for the signal to arrive. The GPS receiver then takes this time and converts it into a distance (just like radar).

GPS is also based on another concept called *triangulation*. In overly simplified terms, triangulation is used to determine where you are if you know how far you are from three different points. For reasons which are beyond the scope of this book, if a GPS receiver receives signals from at least four different GPS satellites, it can determine its location precisely.

Figure 6–12 is a two-dimensional explanation of the (three-dimensional) GPS position determination process. The left side of the figure depicts the situation with a single satellite located at point A. If the receiver knows its distance from point A, then it must be somewhere on the circle (the distance equals the radius). (In a three-dimensional world, this circle is sphere.) On the right side of the figure there is a second satellite at point B. If the receiver knows how far it is from point A and point B, then it must be on both circles, and therefore it must be at one of the two positions shown. When one more satellite is added, the receiver's position is known exactly, as one of the two points is eliminated. As mentioned before, in the real (three-dimensional) world, a fourth satellite is needed to determine position precisely.

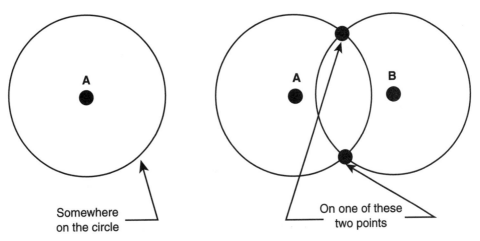

Figure 6–12 Two-dimensional depiction of the GPS location determination process.

Since there are only 21 satellites in the GPS system, they are concentrated around the equator, which means there are places on Earth, near the north and south poles, where less than four satellites are visible at all times. The result is that GPS does not work very well at the ends of the hemispheres (which is why you never hear about Santa Claus using it).

The Next Generation Satellites—LEO

Up until now, I have assumed that all communication satellites are in geosynchronous orbit, which was true until very recently. Today, there are several consortia (which is a fancy word for a group of rich people) working on a new kind of satellite system based on *low Earth orbit* satellites or LEOs. Low Earth orbit satellite systems (called *constellations*) use many small satellites, only a few hundred miles up, to relay RF information.

Why LEOs?

There are several ramifications to using satellites in low Earth orbit. First, the satellites are not stationary with respect to a fixed point on Earth. (If you could see them, they would fly by overhead very quickly.) These non-stationary satellites make communicating with them more complicated than with GEOs. First, RF contact must be made with a moving satellite (which is a challenge in itself). Then, after the RF link is established with the first satellite, it is only a short time before that same satellite is no longer "visible" and an RF connection is no longer possible.

The second ramification of LEO satellites is that because they are so low, they can only project a small antenna footprint (covering a small area), which means that many LEOs are required to fully cover a land area the size of the United States. People on opposite ends of the country, wishing to use LEOs to make contact, will not be able to use the same satellite to connect. All of these ramifications result in a satellite system which is much more complex than a standard, off-the-shelf GEO system.

If LEOs are so complex and require many satellites, why bother? The answer is surprisingly simple: power. LEOs require less RF power to reach than GEOs (which makes sense since they're closer). In fact, some LEOs are low enough to reach with the power in a handheld phone. This is why LEOs are being deployed at all, because they can be reached with the power in a handheld phone, unlike satellites in GEO. LEOs will be used strictly for mobile telephony. They will not be broadcasting your favorite television show any time soon.

Since telephony by LEO is very expensive, it is only meant to be used in places where no other form of mobile telephony (e.g., cellular phones) exists, like out in a desert or in the middle of the ocean. This niche use of an expensive technology has fueled a long running controversy over the soundness of the LEO business. There is one question which everybody is trying to answer: Are there enough customers out in the desert or in the middle of the ocean to pay for the expensive LEO satellite system? Stay tuned.

Did You Know?

Probably the most famous LEO satellite system to date is the Motorola sponsored Iridium system. Iridium was originally designed to use 77 low Earth orbit satellites and it got its name from Iridium, which is the 77th element in the periodic chart of basic elements (remember chemistry?). Sometime into the program however, some bright engineer discovered that the system will work just as well with only 66 satellites, but chose to keep the name Iridium. I guess they figured nobody would ever make a phone call using something called Dysprosium.

How LEOs Work

LEOs work by continuously relaying signals among each other as they move. Figure 6–13 shows generally how a LEO system works. In this example, the satellites are moving counterclockwise. The left side of the figure (Time = 0) shows how a person (located at point 1) on one side of the planet can talk to someone on the other side of the planet (located at point 2) using a LEO system. The phone call, using the LEO's frequency, is transmitted to whichever LEO satellite is closest overhead at that given moment (satellite A on the left side of the figure). That satellite (A) then relays the call to the next closest satellite (B) in the direction of the final destination. This relay process repeats itself until the call reaches the satellite (D) which is over the intended receiver. At that point, the signal is transmitted down with an antenna footprint which encircles the intended receiver. How the system knows which satellites to use at any moment in time is what makes the LEO systems so complex.

After a short period of time (Time = 1 on the right side of Figure 6–13), satellite A will no longer be over the person originating the call (1). It is at this point when satellite A "hands off" the call to satellite B and the process continues as before, only this time the last satellite utilized is no longer D but E. (All of the satellites have rotated counterclockwise.)

The other aspect to know about LEOs is the satellite-power tradeoff. If the LEO satellite system is used with very low-powered handheld phones, then the satellites must be close to Earth (but not so close that they fall on you). The closer to Earth they are, the smaller their footprints will be and, therefore, the more satellites that are required to blanket the whole Earth. And a lot of satellites—even small ones—translates into an expensive system. LEO system designers are constantly trading off between the fewest possible satellites (higher up) and the most user-friendly (low-powered) handheld phones.

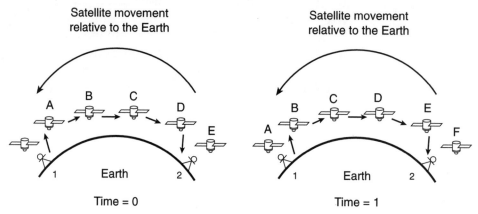

Time = 0   Time = 1

Figure 6–13 Graphical depiction of the workings of a LEO satellite system.

7

The New World of Wireless

If the technology of wireless has been around for a
long time, then what is so new about it? What is new are the myriad of applications which lend themselves to wireless communications as a result of the
tremendous advances made in RF and digital electronics. It took 30 years for
the cellular phone to go from concept to serious market penetration, and
most of that time was spent waiting for the advent of low cost semiconductor
technology to make it financially feasible.

This chapter is a snapshot of the wireless world today (circa 1999), a
world which is in constant transition. Newer technologies continue to replace
older, less efficient ones while new applications for existing technology pop
up everyday. New markets are evolving for this technology as developing
countries seek basic local telephone service and turn to wireless to provide it.
The regulatory landscape is in flux as regulators seek to address the many
challenges—from efficient use of the available spectrum to the coordination
of wireless emergency services.

This chapter is divided into two sections: fixed wireless applications and
mobile telephony. Fixed wireless, as the name implies, is used to describe any
wireless system in which all the parties communicating are stationary. There
are many, many fixed wireless applications, only a few of which are covered
here as a broad overview. One of these applications, point-to-point microwave

communication, is just an enhancement of systems which have been around for years. Most of the enhancement is a result of converting the older, analog technology to the newer, digital technology, the result being that the new (digital) systems can take advantage of digital signal processing (DSP) to cram much more information into a given bandwidth.

Another fixed wireless application, wireless local loop (WLL), in which local telephone service (in the United States) is provided by somebody other than the incumbent local phone company, is a direct result of the FCC opening up the local telephone monopoly to competition.

In this chapter, you will learn about the main topologies used to construct wireless systems. You will also be introduced to a new modulation technique, called spread spectrum, which allows wireless service providers to cram even more users into a given bandwidth.

The section on mobile telephony begins by discussing the plethora of choices available to consumers for these services. You will learn how a generic cellular system works and be exposed to new concepts like handoff, frequency reuse, and air interface. You will also learn about the different technologies which service providers employ to maximize call capacity (and therefore profits).

Today, the demand for wireless connectivity all over the world has outpaced the supply (which should give you a clue as to where to invest). I have heard it said that 25% of the people on the planet die without ever making a phone call. Ignoring for the moment those people who actually have nobody to call, wireless technology offers the fastest and most cost effective way to allow these people to "reach out and touch someone." The world is just beginning to feel the enormous impact of wireless communications. Increased bandwidth demand for everything from wireless Internet access to wireless videoconferencing will ensure that every megahertz of spectrum is fully utilized.

FIXED WIRELESS APPLICATIONS ....

Point-to-Point Microwave

What is Point-to-Point Microwave?

Point-to-point microwave, sometimes called microwave relay, has been around since the mid 1940s. Of course, back then, microwave relay was analog, meaning it used analog modulation to combine the information signal and the RF carrier. What makes point-to-point microwaves new is the use of digital modulation and the new ways in which it is being used.

Point-to-point microwave, as the name implies, is used to communicate, wirelessly, between a single transmitter and a single receiver, both owned by the same entity. This point is important, because when someone is given the right (by the FCC) to communicate using point-to-point microwaves at a certain frequency and in a certain geographical location, everyone else is prohibited from using that frequency in that location. In this respect, it is similar to broadcasting. As you will soon see, there are point-to-point wireless applications where this limitation does not hold.

The tremendous advantage of point-to-point microwave is the user's ability to get information from one point to another without owning the underlying real estate.

Uses for Point-to-Point Microwave

The FCC has allocated many frequency bands for this application, and for many different uses, but by far there are three uses which dominate all others. The first of these uses is referred to as private operational fixed microwave. Most often, the owner of the transmitter and receiver is a private company. In these cases, the wireless systems are used to control (an unattended piece of equipment), to monitor (temperature, pressure, voltage, etc.), or to relay (voice, data, fax, etc.). These systems are especially useful along right-of-ways like highways and railroads.

A second use for point-to-point is relaying large volumes of voice traffic called common carrier microwave. This is one of the ways in which long distance telephone companies get calls from here to there. As will be discussed in the next section, this application is also used by mobile telephony providers to get the phone call from the basestation back to the home office. Common carrier microwave is often used when the terrain over which the signal must travel is severe and laying copper wire (or optical fibers) is impractical.

The third main use for point-to-point microwave is video relay and is referred to as broadcast auxiliary microwave. This is the way in which mobile TV news vans get their signals back to the station. It is also the way the television stations get their signals up to their broadcast antennas, as previously discussed and detailed in Figure 6–4.

Did You Know?

Private microwave relay is how the long distance carrier MCI came into being. Back in the early 1960s, a man named Jack Goeken set up a series of microwave relays between Chicago and St. Louis to help his customers keep track of their merchandise on the way to market. One day he had a brainstorm. Those same relays could be used to provide long distance telephony. That insight led to a 20-year battle that ended with the breakup of AT&T.

Point-to-Point Operations

As mentioned above, microwave relay is used in places where laying copper or optical fibers makes no sense or is impossible, but there is a limit. Our old friend, line-of-sight, ensures that microwave relays are spaced no more than 25 miles apart, which means if a signal is to be transmitted from Los Angeles to San Diego (about 120 miles) using point-to-point microwave communications, at least four microwave relay stations are required. A microwave relay tower with directional antennas is shown in Figure 7–1.

The first thing to notice in Figure 7–1 is that microwave relays use dish antennas (which are covered in this picture for environmental reasons). Recall that dish antennas are highly directional (their antenna pattern has a narrow beamwidth). This makes sense as the microwave relay wants as much RF energy as possible going in only one direction (toward the next receiver). In some instances, microwave relays use horn antennas (shaped like square funnels) to cover wider bandwidths. Most point-to-point communication takes place at high enough frequencies to allow the use of small dish antennas.

As much as the RF system designers desire that *all* of the RF energy go from one relay to the next, it doesn't. Instead, as the RF energy leaves one re-

Figure 7–1   A point-to-point microwave tower. *Courtesy of Andrew Corp.*

lay, the energy spreads out, like water coming out of a hose. Some of the RF energy goes directly to the next relay, some goes off into space, and some bounces off the ground. If that were the end of the story, everything would be fine. Unfortunately, some of the RF energy which bounces off of the ground also makes its way to the next relay, as shown in Figure 7–2. Since the reflected signal has further to travel, it arrives at the next relay later than the direct signal. This situation is called *multipath*, and it is very similar to the situation in broadcasting in which signals reflect off buildings and cause ghost images in television reception. As a result, sophisticated techniques have been developed to eliminate this problem.

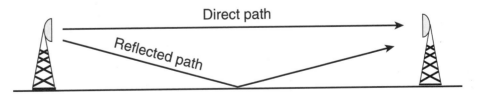

Figure 7–2   Graphical depiction of the multipath effect.

Most of today's high volume point-to-point microwave communications, primarily long distance voice traffic, use digital modulation. The reasons are twofold. First, the RF electronics have become sophisticated enough to implement digital microwave communication. And second, digital modulation allows for cramming more information (more simultaneous telephone conversations) into a given bandwidth. Microwave point-to-point frequency allocations run as low as a few megahertz up to and beyond 38 GHz.

Wireless Local Loop

What is the Local Loop?

In the United States, when you pick up your telephone to make a call, you hear a dial tone, which means you are connected to what is referred to as a Class 5 switching center, also called the end office. You are now connected to your local telephone company. The electrical circuit between you, the end office, and back again is affectionately referred to as the *local loop*. Whether you know it or not, today (circa 1999) there is a battle being waged over control of the local loop.

Basically, there are only four ways to reach the local telephone company's end office (i.e., there are only four ways to implement the local loop.): copper wire, coaxial cable, fiber optic cable, and wireless communication.

The copper is owned by the local phone company and they try to cram as much information down that poor little piece of wire as is technologically possible. The coaxial cable is owned by the local cable company (if you are lucky enough to have one). They too are trying to cram as much information as is technologically possible down the cable. Today, running fiber optic cable to individual homes is considered infeasible. And then there is wireless.

Why Wireless Local Loop?

In the battle for local loop supremacy, wireless local loop (WLL) is proving to be a very formidable competitor. Wireless local loop technology is simultaneously addressing two very different markets. One market which WLL is addressing is local telephone service in developing nations who do not yet have it, like China and Vietnam. In places such as these, wireless technology is much less expensive and far faster to deploy than laying copper wires in the ground. All of the major wireless infrastructure manufacturers are aggressively pursuing WLL business in developing countries.

The other market being addressed by WLL is in the United States. Why would anyone need WLL in a country where almost everyone has hard-wired local telephone service? Two reasons. First, long distance telephone companies want more than anything else to be local telephone companies too. And they can be, immediately, if they want, but they have to use the local telephone company's equipment and pay them a fee, which sort of defeats the purpose. Wireless local loop technology allows long distance telephone companies to deploy telephone equipment, at a fraction of the cost of laying copper wire, and compete directly with the local telephone companies for local phone business. And with the growth of the Internet, an increasing amount of phone time is considered "local." WLL will some day soon offer most people an alternative to local phone service, probably from their long distance provider.

The other reason for WLL in the United States is increased bandwidth. Everyone wants high speed access to the Internet, and high speed means more bandwidth. There is only so much information that can be stuffed down a copper wire or a coaxial cable, and if more bandwidth is desired than either of them can supply, it must come from somewhere else. And until someone figures out how to lay fiber optic cable inexpensively, the only other solution is wireless, and more specifically, WLL.

Wireless Local Loop Technology

Wireless local loop systems, as envisioned, will generally divide a geographic region into a number of similar sized cells (like cellular telephony). Each cell will be serviced by a basestation, which will communicate with all of the wireless local loop customers within the cell. The basestation may be as simple as a small omnidirectional antenna and control box hanging from the overhead electrical lines. Each customer will be equipped with a transceiver and a small patch antenna. The transceiver may have several outputs: one for a telephone, one for a modem, and maybe even one for a television. The small antenna, which may be inside or outside, will be positioned to communicate with the basestation.

What equipment and frequencies will WLL use? It depends. If the system is to provide basic local telephone service to a developing nation, then the bandwidth requirements will be modest, and almost any infrastructure at any frequency will do. The major wireless infrastructure manufacturers, who provide the systems for mobile telephony, are naturally trying to use that same equipment for WLL to avoid having to develop anything new. Most of the WLL in underdeveloped countries will ultimately be at the same frequencies as the mobile telephony in developed countries and will utilize the same basic equipment, only slimmed down to provide fixed service only.

The Perfect WLL Solution—LMDS

If the WLL system is intended to provide broadband connectivity in the United States, then the bandwidth requirements are more substantial and just any old frequency allocation will not do. However, the FCC has allocated a special frequency band which is tailor-made for WLL called *local multipoint distribution service*, or LMDS, that resides between 27 and 31 GHz.

The LMDS frequency band was not specifically allocated for WLL. The owner of the frequency band (in a given geographic area) can use it for almost any application. However, there is something very special about the A Block frequency allocation. (LMDS is divided into two different frequency bands: A Block and B Block.) The A Block frequency allocation for LMDS is 1150 MHz wide, which makes it the widest allocated frequency band (by the FCC) in the history of the United States. And since frequency is like real estate (they ain't makin' any more of it), the LMDS A Block is one of the most valuable commodities in the wireless world today.

Did You Know?

The LMDS frequency allocations, like every other frequency allocation today, was auctioned off by the FCC to the highest bidders in early 1999. The auctions raised about $45 million, which is not very much when you consider it gives the winners the ability to compete with the local telephone company, the local cable company, and the Internet service providers. This is probably the result of price shock from previous wireless auctions in which the bidders, getting caught up in all the excitement, bid exorbitant amounts of money. You gotta pay to play.

To get an appreciation for how substantial 1150 MHz of wireless spectrum is, a telephone conversation requires 4 kHz of bandwidth (uncompressed), which means the LMDS A Block can simultaneously transmit over a quarter of a million phone calls. Now you know why most owners are opting to use it for WLL. (Do you think the major long distance carriers might be interested in LMDS?)

Just so you don't think that LMDS is a perfect solution for WLL, it is not without its hurdles to overcome. First, RF electronics at 31 GHz is still relatively expensive, both on the system side and the consumer side. Second, if you recall something from a previous chapter called absorption, you will remember that it limits the distance an RF wave can travel and that the higher the frequency, the worse it gets. Well, at 31 GHz (LMDS's frequency), it is pretty bad. Signal attenuation from absorption (at 31 GHz) requires the receiver to be relatively close to the basestation's transmitter to make use of the LMDS band. That means in a given geographical area there needs to be a lot of basestations for the system to work properly, and a lot of basestations translates to an expensive system. And I won't even mention what happens to a 31 GHz signal during a torrential downpour.

Before you get depressed and give up on LMDS, the systems will begin to appear soon and most will be deployed for wireless local loop. Unfortunately, it will probably not be available at your home anytime soon, because the owners of these expensive LMDS systems actually intend to get a return on their investment. (Can you believe it?) What that means is that the first LMDS systems to appear will most likely be for small businesses (with big wallets), with basestations located near business parks which provide telephone and high speed Internet access. This will serve as the first implementation, in the United States, of wireless local loop.

A New Technology—Spread Spectrum

ISM—Unlicensed Spread Spectrum

The FCC has allocated several frequency bands to applications which are collectively known as *industrial, scientific, and medical,* or ISM. ISM applications include everything from industrial heating equipment to microwave ovens. What ISM does not include—or it did not include until recently—is wireless communications. The ISM bands were originally intended to allow various electrical and mechanical equipment to radiate unintentional RF energy (at specified frequencies), without interfering with other wireless communication applications. As long as the industrial applications and the wireless applications are operating in their own frequency bands, they don't interfere with each other.

Surprisingly enough, the ISM bands now provide an opportunity for wireless communications. If nothing else, wireless communications operating in an ISM band certainly won't have to worry that their signals will interfere with existing applications. (Microwave ovens don't mind listening in on wireless conversations.) The only problem is, how is it possible to communicate wirelessly in a frequency band with so much unintentional RF energy being radiated? The answer is something called *spread spectrum.*

Spread spectrum is a technique which allows RF circuitry to distinguish one signal from another when both are operating at the exact same carrier frequency and in the same geographical location. After the development of spread spectrum technology, the FCC recognized an opportunity to make more spectrum available by opening up the ISM bands to wireless communications. And because the FCC is so generous, they decided that as long as their rules are obeyed, no license is needed to operate a wireless system. Operating a wireless system in an ISM band, while transmitting less than one watt, is referred to as *unlicensed spread spectrum*, which is a very unique wireless application. It is one of the only (if not the only) fixed, point-to-point wireless applications which has different users sharing the same frequency in the same geographical location. Spread spectrum technology is what allows each party to distinguish their signals from the other parties'. Table 7–1 shows the three most popular ISM frequency bands.

Table 7–1   ISM Frequency Bands

Frequency Band	Frequency Allocation
UHF	902–928 MHz
S-band	2.40–2.50 GHz
C-band	5.725–5.875 GHz

Did You Know?

Spread spectrum technology has actually been around for some time. The military has been using it to encode wireless transmissions for secure communications for many years. The reason it has begun to appear in the commercial arena is more a result of the availability of low cost electronics than of any breakthrough in technology.

Spread Spectrum—Theory of Operation

Recall the analogy of wireless communications being like mailing a letter. In this analogy, the letter is the information signal and the envelope is the RF carrier signal. Modulation is used to combine the letter (information) and the envelope (the carrier). In the previous discussion of point-to-point wireless communications, I assumed that only one party could transmit and receive at a given frequency within a given geographical location. In that version of the analogy, there was no need to address the envelope, because there was only one party who could receive it. (Maybe there was only one other house in the neighborhood.) This is not the case with spread spectrum. With spread spectrum, many parties can transmit and receive at a given frequency within a given geographical location. (There are a lot of houses in the neighborhood and they can all mail letters to each other.) How does spread spectrum ensure that the "envelope" finds its correct destination? It uses an "address."

Spread spectrum is analogous to imprinting an address onto the wireless signal. How does spread spectrum pull off this little magic trick? It modulates the signal *again*. There are two flavors of spread spectrum. One is called *direct sequence spread spectrum* or DSSS, and the other one is called *frequency hopping spread spectrum* or FHSS.

In DSSS, the spread spectrum modulation takes place while the original information signal is still in digital form. (By the way, did I neglect to mention that spread spectrum only works with a digital information signal?) In this case, the party transmitting the signal has a special code, which is nothing more than another digital signal. This (digital) code is used to modulate the (digital) information signal. (Think of it as multiplying the information signal by a secret number.) The trick to using spread spectrum is that the receiving party has the complimentary code. When they receive the signal, they multiply it by their own (complimentary) secret number. What results is the same information signal which was originally transmitted. There are a lot of other parties that receive the same signal, but they all have a different code (i.e., they multiply by a different secret number.) What they receive is undecipherable and therefore ignored.

FSSS is similar to DSSS, except in this case the transmitted carrier frequency is instantaneously and continuously changed according to the special code. Since the receiver also has the same code, it knows what frequencies to look for when receiving. All the other receivers, which have a different code and are therefore looking for completely different frequencies, do not "see" the transmitted signal.

Spread spectrum gets its name from the fact that modulating the signal with the special code "spreads" the bandwidth of the signal over a wider bandwidth. For instance, the human voice requires 4 kHz of bandwidth. After it is modulated with the special code, however, it might cover 4 MHz. The same voice information is still there; it just covers a wider frequency range. After the process is reversed, the signal will return to its original 4 kHz bandwidth.

ISM Spread Spectrum Applications

Because no license is required, spread spectrum in the ISM bands is finding all kinds of applications. One of the most common is cordless telephones. The latest generation of digital cordless phones utilizes spread spectrum in the 900 MHz and 2.4 GHz bands. The great (theoretical) advantage is the lack of interference from other forms of RF radiation. (The phone completely ignores the microwave oven.)

There is at least one company using the ISM band for point-to-point communication. In this case, they put two highly directional antennas (facing each other) on top of towers or street lights, separated by some distance, and use the signal to transmit information. Because the power is limited to one watt, the signal cannot travel as far as licensed point-to-point communications, so this application is limited to relatively short distances.

Another growing application for the ISM band is *wireless local area networks* or WLAN. (A local area network or LAN is a group of computers in the same location which communicate with each other.) This strategy involves using an omnidirectional antenna, at the server, to cover the entire area of the local area network. In this way, all the computers within the WLAN are assigned their own special code to communicate directly with the server. This application is ideal as the one watt output limitation is sufficient to cover the area of most local area networks.

Finally, the ISM band is being used for wireless local loop (WLL), but not in the way you might think. It is not being used to deliver high bandwidth or even local telephone service to the home. Instead, it is being used by utility companies to read gas, electric, and water meters. In these systems, a basestation transceiver is located somewhere in the neighborhood (maybe on a telephone pole) and is used to periodically communicate with a wireless transceiver installed in the home's meters. If you do not have this feature installed in your home at present, just wait, you will.

Other Applications

FCC Allocations

The FCC continues to allocate (and auction off) bandwidth for wireless applications. Some of these allocations are so new that the auctions are still being conducted (circa 1999) and will continue to be conducted into the foreseeable future. In many instances, the FCC has remained flexible as to the end use of the actual bandwidth itself. Table 7–2 contains a sampling of some of the newer wireless allocations (and applications). Strictly speaking, these are not all fixed wireless applications. In most cases, there is flexibility to provide either fixed or mobile wireless service.

Table 7–2 Some Newer Wireless Applications

Acronym	Wireless Service	Frequency Band	Possible Uses
GWCS	General Wireless Communication Service	4660–4685 MHz	Fixed or mobile communications.
LMS	Location and Monitoring Service	904–927 MHz	To determine the location of mobile radio units.
MMDS	Multichannel Multipoint Communication Service	2596–2690 MHz	Broadcasting.
WCS	Wireless Communication Services	2345 -2360 MHz	Fixed, mobile, radio location, or satellite communications.

One of the implications of this flexibility in end use for these new services is that there may not be a consensus, across the entire country, as to what is implemented. This might severely limit the utility of these new allocations. One of the reasons that cellular phones are so useful is that the entire country uses the same frequency bands for cellular communications. This means that the same cellular phone which works in Los Angeles will also work in Iowa. (Which is pretty useful, if you have to be in Iowa.) This same utility will not exist if the new wireless service providers all decide to implement something different in their geographical location.

If you build it, they will come, does not necessarily apply to wireless applications. Just because somebody has won the right to provide a wireless service does not mean that anybody really wants it (or is willing to pay for it). A prime example is MMDS (see Table 7–2). MMDS was originally slated for wireless cable TV; the idea being to provide the same programming as the local cable provider, only wirelessly. The service provider transmits the programming in the MMDS band from a tower situated at the highest point in the area. To use the service, the consumer would only need to have a small antenna and a TV set top box, and of course pay the monthly fee. The hope was to foster competition to the cable providers, resulting in lower prices for the consumer.

A funny thing happened on the way to wireless (MMDS) cable—nobody (in the U.S.) wanted it. The bad news, for those trying to deploy MMDS, was that right around the time MMDS was coming into being, direct broadcast satellite began to take off and those consumers who were motivated to change, typically went that route. So presently in the United States sits 200 MHz of unused spectrum which somebody is trying to find a use for. The good news for MMDS is that the United States is only part of the equation. In developing countries (those without direct broadcast satellite), MMDS has found a receptive audience.

MOBILE TELEPHONY ....

Mobile Telephony Choices

Different Technologies

There are several choices for mobile telephone service in the United States. Some of these services differentiate themselves by offering additional features compared to "standard" mobile service, while others are the natural evolution of technology over time, taking advantage of newer digital technology.

One of the lesser known mobile services available is something called *Specialized Mobile Radio* or SMR. SMR, which operates in two different frequency bands between 806 and 866 MHz, was originally intended for use as a wireless dispatch service (think taxi cabs). Today, it has evolved into a combination dispatch and mobile phone service. This combination service distinguishes SMR from all the other mobile phone services available. Not only can the service be used to make "ordinary" mobile calls in the interconnected mode, it can also be used to conduct wireless teleconferencing in dispatch mode. In this mode, several people using the service can hold a conversation simultaneously. As such, SMR is popular with teams of mobile salespeople who need to conduct spontaneous sales conferences.

The mobile phone service which most people in the U.S. are familiar with, and the one most often referred to as *cellular*, is something called *Advanced Mobile Phone Service* or AMPS. AMPS is an analog technology, using frequency modulation, and it is often referred to as first generation cellular technology. AMPS operates in two bands between 824 and 894 MHz. The reason for the two bands is that two different service providers are able to offer cellular service in a given area. The FCC allocated two bands to foster competition, resulting in better pricing for consumers.

The best feature of first generation cellular service is that every service provider throughout the United States uses (or used) the same modulation scheme. This uniformity has led to the concept of roaming (using a cellular phone outside its home area), in which one cellular phone can be used everywhere. The bad news is that it used analog technology, which you should know by now cannot handle the same capacity of phone calls as digital technology and, as such, the analog systems quickly ran out of capacity (think busy signals).

This capacity problem caused service providers to update their systems to the newer digital technology, which provides much more capacity (think profits). These new digital cellular systems are referred to as second generation cellular technology. The good news with the digital technology is that you are much more likely to be able to complete a call in high usage areas. Unfortunately, these upgraded systems led to some unforeseen problems.

The older analog systems did not get upgraded to digital systems instantly. For some period of time, most service providers had (or have) a hybrid system: part analog and part digital. This led to the creation of the *dual mode* phone. These (expensive) dual mode phones can communicate in both analog and digital (and switch between the two). Of course, to take advantage of the new technology, somebody (you) has to go out and buy a new mobile phone.

By far the biggest problem with upgrading to digital technology stems from the fact that there is more than one digital modulation scheme to choose from. Many of the service providers chose different technologies, for different reasons. You may have already guessed the problem. The roaming feature which is so universal in analog cellular systems is not quite so universal in digital cellular systems. As you will soon learn, there are really only two digital technologies vying for supremacy in the United States. As a result, as long as the two competitors in a given area use these two different technologies, you are assured that your digital phone will work (with at least one of them) in that area while roaming.

Another second generation mobile phone service is called *Personal Communications Services* or PCS. PCS, or more specifically wideband PCS, is nothing more than second generation (digital) cellular technology at a slightly higher frequency. PCS operates in six bands between 1850 and 1980 MHz. The FCC allocated six different bands to spur competition and to offer entrepreneurs an opportunity to play in the mobile telephone game.

Did You Know?

After realizing the error of their ways in the cellular lottery, the FCC began auctioning off bandwidth for wireless services. The auction for PCS alone netted over ten billion (that's with a "b") dollars. The fact that many of the "winners" did not actually have the money to pay up is another story altogether. You live and learn.

If you have been paying attention, you have observed that in most areas in the United States there are (or will be) *10* different choices for mobile telephone service (2 SMR, 2 cellular, and 6 PCS), not counting satellite-based mobile telephony. The question everyone is asking—or should be asking—is, can the market support 10 different mobile telephone service providers? Who will survive? Stay tuned.

A World of Choices

Just so you do not get the wrong idea, the United States is far from being the only place with mobile telephony. Table 7–3 shows some of the world's major mobile telephone systems. The first thing to notice is that there are a lot of different digital technologies vying for international supremacy. The way things stand today, digital phones which work in the United States will not work anywhere else and vice versa, which can be a problem for those traveling internationally. The good news is that there may be a solution right around the corner.

Table 7–3   Worldwide Mobile Telephone Systems

Acronym	System	Where First Deployed	Technology
AMPS	Advanced Mobile Telephone Service	United States	Analog
CDMA	Code Division Multiple Access	United States	Digital
D-AMPS	Digital Advanced Mobile Telephone Service	United States	Digital
DCS1800	Digital Communication Service	Germany & England	Digital
GSM	Group Special Mobile	80 European countries	Digital

Table 7–3 Worldwide Mobile Telephone Systems (Continued)

Acronym	System	Where First Deployed	Technology
JTACS	Japan Total Access Communications System	Japan	Analog
NADC	North American Digital Cellular	United States	Digital
NMT	Nordic Mobile Telephone	Scandinavian countries	Analog
PCS1900	Personal Communications Services	United States	Digital
PDC	Personal Digital Cellular	Japan	Digital
SMR	Specialized Mobile Radio	United States	Both
TACS	Total Access Communications System	England	Analog

The Next Generation

Somebody got the idea that it would be really nice if there were a single digital technology deployed worldwide which allowed the use of a single mobile phone anywhere in the world (which has service). In steps the International Telecommunications Union ITU. The ITU is the FCC of the world, with responsibility for allocating "international" frequencies. The ITU, along with all the member nations, have started a program called IMT-2000 (International Mobile Telephone). The goal of the program is to develop a single, digital standard which will work all over the world. IMT-2000, which will offer true international mobility, is affectionately referred to as the third generation cellular, or 3G, technology and is situated between 1885 and 2200 MHz.

The two digital technologies which have emerged as the prominent contenders for IMT-2000 are CDMA and GSM (see Table 7–3). The good news is that the two companies backing these technologies (Qualcomm in the United States for CDMA and Ericsson in Sweden for GSM) have begun to cooperate and work together to fulfill the ITU's vision of international mobile telephony. Stay tuned.

The Cellular Concept

Topology

The United States is broken down into a multitude of geographical regions in which the various forms of mobile telephony are authorized. Within the cellular allocation, the United States is broken down into metropolitan statistical areas or MSAs (think city) and rural statistical areas or RSAs (think country). There are two—or, in the case of PCS, six—service providers authorized to provide mobile telephony in each of these areas. The service providers distinguish themselves by being allotted different frequency subbands within the overall cellular frequency allotment. Within their assigned geographical region, each service provider breaks up their area into smaller segments called cells.

Each of these cells has an antenna (or antennas) at the center of the cell which projects an antenna pattern, or footprint, covering the entire cell. These antenna patterns provide transmitting and receiving coverage for users within it. Because of the nature of RF behavior, these antenna footprints are circular in shape. However, when RF engineers display a cell pattern on a map, they ordinarily use hexagons to describe the antenna footprints. It is not that hexagons more accurately reflect the antenna patterns, it is that hexagons fit together very nicely into an orderly pattern (see Figure 7–3).

In the world of mobile telephony, there is one major tradeoff constantly taking place. Ideally, the system has a large number of very small hexagons. As you will soon learn, the greater the number of hexagons, the more simultaneous calls the system can handle (think revenue). However, the larger the number of hexagons, the greater the infrastructure required to implement the system (think expenses). As a result, cell coverage is a dynamic activity which is constantly changing in response to increases in capacity requirements.

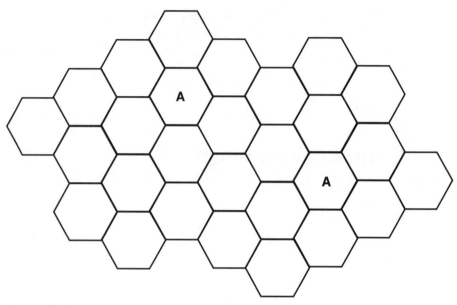

Figure 7–3   Cell pattern covering a geographic area.

Cells come in three basic sizes: macrocells, microcells, and picocells. There are no exact definitions for each of these except to say that macros are bigger than micros, which are bigger than picos. Macro cells are representative of the first generation cellular systems. Micro cells and pico cells are new developments which have resulted from the subdividing of macrocells to add capacity.

Infrastructure

At the center of every cell is a *cell site* or *basestation*. The cell site contains all of the electronics which enable wireless communication, including all of the RF hardware. At a minimum, cell sites consist of one or more antennas, cables, a transmitter and receiver, a power source, and other control electronics. If the capacity requirements of the cell are small, the cell may employ a single omnidirectional antenna to provide coverage. In situations where more capacity is required, the cell is broken down into three sectors (120 degrees each) and one or more antennas are used to provide coverage for each sector. This is the familiar triangular-top tower often seen by the side of the road and shown previously in Figure 3–5.

At their very simplest, all cell sites provide three functions. Cell sites talk to each other (think mobile to mobile calls), they connect to the public switched telephone network or PSTN (think mobile to landline calls), and they count how many minutes you talk (think money). All three of these functions take place at something called a *mobile switching center* or MSC, also referred to as a *mobile telephone switching office* or MTSO.

The MSC is the quarterback for a cellular system. It acts as a hub through which all cellular calls are routed. Figure 7–4 shows a cellular system configuration and the role of the MSC.

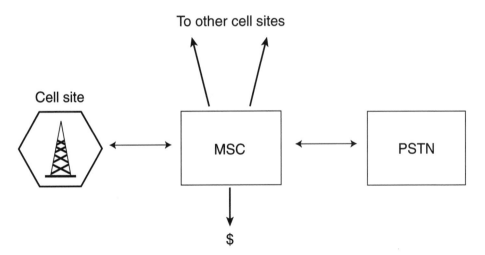

Figure 7–4 *Cellular system configuration.*

As can be seen in Figure 7–4, the MSC is directly connected to each cell site and to the PSTN. When a call is made, it gets routed from the current cell to the MSC and then onto the PSTN (if the other person is on a landline phone) or to another cell (if the other person is on a mobile phone)—and all the while the cash register at the MSC is ringing away.

The MSC is connected to the PSTN by a very high capacity telephone connection. The MSC is connected to each cell site by one of three methods. It uses either a high capacity copper telephone line (called a T1 line), a fiber optic cable, or a point-to-point microwave relay (as discussed in the previous section). The choice of which method is used depends on several things, including the particular cell site's traffic level, how far way the cell is from the MSC, and the terrain between them.

Mobility

The feature which separates mobile telephony from most other wireless applications is the notion that the mobile unit must be able to change what it communicates with dynamically. In fixed wireless communications, there are two transceivers used to establish a single communication link and they remain unchanged during the entire event. In mobile telephony, the mobile transceiver must be constantly changing between transceivers (located at different cell sites) it communicates with as it moves.

Cell sites continuously transmit out a control signal to all the mobile units within their cell. When a mobile phone is first turned on, it shortly receives this control signal and responds by transmitting one of its own. Several cell sites within the area receive this response from the mobile, not just the cell it is in. The key to mobile telephony is power level discrimination. All of the cell sites receive the mobile unit's response, but they all receive different power levels; the cell which receives the highest power response is the cell where the mobile is. Step one is complete: the MSC knows where the mobile unit is.

When the mobile attempts to make a call, it is allocated a small frequency band within the cell to conduct the call. During the call, the signal level (power) is constantly monitored by the MSC by way of the cell site. As the signal level drops, the MSC knows that the mobile is getting ready to leave that cell and enter another cell. Keep in mind that the control signal is still being received by multiple cell sites. It is at this point that the MSC looks to see which adjacent cell site is receiving the most powerful control signal; that cell site is the one which is going to get the call next. How does it make the transition?

At the appropriate time, the MSC conducts an operation called *handoff*. The handoff process is what is known as a make-before-break connection. In essence, the mobile phone is communicating with two different cell sites for a brief period of time during the handoff. (Otherwise parts of conversations are missing.) This handoff process has its advantages and disadvantages. On the one hand, it provides true mobility. On the other hand, it ties up two cell sites for one call (think lower profits). More will be discussed about this in the next section.

Frequency Reuse and Air Interface

Frequency Reuse

The goal of every mobile telephone service provider is to conduct as many simultaneous calls as possible (think greed). In most wireless technologies, only one party is permitted to transmit a signal, at a given frequency, in a defined geographical location, which works fine for applications like broadcasting. (Having two different stations simultaneously transmitting channel six would really cause a headache.) But cellular technology is different.

In the United States, each cellular provider is allocated 25 MHz of spectrum, 12.5 MHz for transmitting (called the downstream) and 12.5 MHz for receiving (called the upstream). Cellular telephony is a *duplex* system—both parties can talk at the same time (think husband and wife) because transmitting and receiving are allocated their own frequencies.

In first generation cellular (AMPS) each phone conversation is allocated 30 kHz of spectrum. Therefore, each 12.5 MHz of bandwidth can handle 416 simultaneous phone calls as shown in Figure 7–5. If the cellular service providers were to follow the broadcast model, only 416 total calls could be conducted simultaneously in a given geographical area (an MSA or RSA). Letting only 416 people talk at once in, say, Southern California, would not even satisfy the demands of Beverly Hills.

The good news is that there is no need for cellular service to follow the broadcast model. Since a person on a mobile call only needs their allocated frequency *within* the cell they are currently in, there is no reason somebody else on the other end of town cannot be using that same exact frequency in an entirely different cell. The concept of multiple users operating at the same frequency, at the same time, and in the same geographic area, is called *frequency reuse*, and it is what separates mobile telephony from fixed wireless communications.

For frequency reuse to work properly it is imperative that each cell phone only put out enough power to reach the cell site of the cell it is in. If it puts out too much power, it will not only reach the intended cell site, it will reach unintended cell sites, which others may be using at the same frequency for a totally different conversation. This limitation on transmitted power, however, is also an advantage in that low power transmission means that the cellular phone's battery charge will last longer.

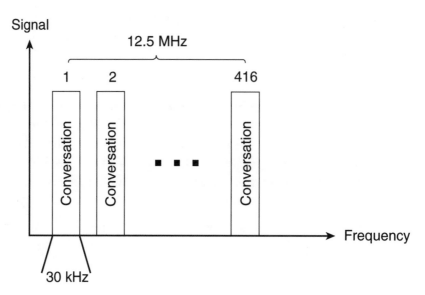

Figure 7–5   *Frequency allocation in the AMPS.*

Referring back to Figure 7–3, users located in the cells marked with the letter A can both be using the same exact frequency to conduct their own separate conversations. Here is a challenging question: how come *adjacent* cells cannot conduct different conversations at the same frequency (and the same time)? Imagine that you are a cellular caller on the border between cells and you are communicating with one cell site, but the power level received at the other cell site is almost as great, causing interference to anyone using that frequency in that cell. Because of this potential interference, identical frequencies in adjacent cells cannot be used simultaneously.

One again there is a tradeoff to be made. To avoid the possibility of interference, cells using the same frequency at the same time must be as far away as possible. Conversely, if the cellular provider wants to make as much money as possible (and they do), the cells must be as close together as possible, so more people can talk simultaneously. In practice, the number of cells of separation, which depends on many things, ranges anywhere from four to 21.

Air Interface

As mentioned above, in AMPS each 12.5 MHz of bandwidth is broken down by frequency into 416 different channels, with one conversation per channel. This dividing up of the frequency band is known as *frequency division multiple access* or FDMA. For AMPS, having 416 different possible conversations at one time (in a given cell) is fine, but what if there were a way to get more than 416 possible simultaneous conversations at one time out of the same 12.5 MHz frequency allocation? With the new digital technologies available, there is.

There are two ways which the new digital wireless technology can increase conversation capacity, and they are referred to as *air interfaces*. Think of air interface as a second modulation of the RF signal which takes advantage of digital technology to increase capacity.

The first of these air interfaces is known as *time division multiple access* or TDMA. TDMA takes the same 30 kHz bandwidth which AMPS uses and breaks it down into time slots, as shown in Figure 7–6. Notice that the horizontal axis is labeled with "time." Several conversations can take place simultaneously in the same frequency band because each conversation is periodically allocated a short time slot in which to transmit its message. This obviously requires some sophisticated signal processing, but it does result in higher cell site capacity. Theoretically, each channel can be broken down into six different time slots, which increases the call carrying capacity of the system sixfold.

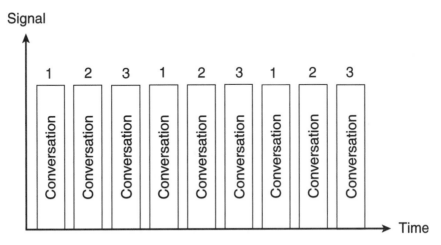

Figure 7–6   *Time division multiple access.*

The other air interface is known as *code division multiple access* or CDMA. Recall from the previous section on fixed wireless applications, I mentioned a technology called spread spectrum. In essence, spread spectrum stamps an RF signal with a destination address. In this manner, many signals can coexist in the same frequency band at the same time, which is how CDMA operates. In fact, it is a form of direct sequence spread spectrum (DSSS). And because of the miracle of digital technology, more conversations can be crammed into a given bandwidth with CDMA than any other currently employed technology. Figure 7–7 is a graphical depiction of CDMA.

Referring to Figure 7–7, when the RF signal has the CDMA "address" imprinted on it, the spectrum it occupies gets bigger. For instance, a signal which occupies 30 kHz before the address is applied might occupy 1 MHz after the address is applied. This "spreading" of the occupied frequency is why it is called spread spectrum. At first thought, it might seem that having a signal occupy more frequency than it does in its original form is a mistake. However, even though it does occupy a greater frequency band than in its original form, the system can now pile many signals on top of each other because they can all be distinguished by their "address." In this manner, more *total* signals can fit into a given frequency band, and that is, after all, the goal of every service provider.

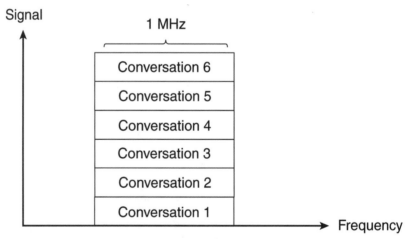

Figure 7–7   Code division multiple access.

The two major air interfaces used predominantly today are IS-95 for CDMA and GSM for TDMA. IS-95 is more or less the brainchild of Qualcomm Inc. in the United States, while GSM is a technology proffered by Ericsson in Sweden. The goal of the third generation cellular (3G) is to find a way to combine the best of both IS-95 and GSM. Good luck.

Adding Capacity

Within a Cell

Even with all the advances in digital technology macrocells eventually run out of call capacity. (Let's face it, people like to chat.) The service providers like this because it means their cellular infrastructure is being utilized to its fullest. Consumers, on the other hand, get frustrated when they try to make a mobile call and they are greeted with a busy signal. When macrocells run out of call carrying capacity, the only thing the service providers can do—if they want to keep their customers—is to subdivide the macrocell into smaller microcells, as shown in Figure 7–8.

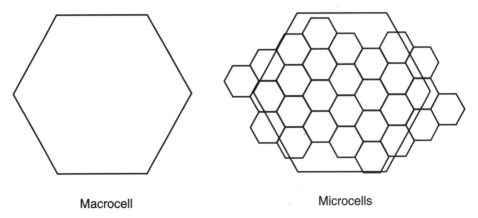

Macrocell   Microcells

Figure 7–8   *Dividing up a macrocell into microcells.*

When subdividing a macrocell into microcells each microcell must be capable of communicating directly with the MSC, which means laying copper wire or fiber optic cable or, more frequently, setting up a point-to-point microwave connection. In any event, replacing a macrocell with several microcells is an expensive proposition and the expense must be justified. As a result, microcells only appear in well-traveled corridors, like along a busy freeway.

Occasionally, it even makes sense to further subdivide a microcell into smaller picocells, where mobile traffic is highly concentrated, like a common area in a large city (think Times Square).

Uncovered Areas

When mobile telephone service providers begin to roll out their systems, they naturally place the first macrocells in the highest traffic areas, which means even after the service is up and running there are still areas within the service provider's territory which may not have service. The two places which get call coverage last are the outer fringes of the service provider's territory and places within the territory which suffer from some sort of obstruction. The latter is comprised of tunnels, subways, and the insides of buildings.

The general category of product used to extend a macrocell's coverage is called a *repeater*. Repeaters come in many shapes and sizes but they all perform one basic function: they extend the wireless range of a macrocell. In that vein, they communicate directly with the macrocell either via copper, fiber optics, or a wireless link. Figure 7–9 shows the layout of a system using a macrocell and a repeater to reach automobiles within a tunnel.

Functionally, there is a very significant difference between using a repeater to extend capacity and breaking down macrocells into microcells to increase capacity. Microcells add capacity because each microcell communicates directly with the MSC. Repeaters, because they communicate with the macrocell itself, actually take away capacity from the macrocell. Every person using the repeater's capacity inside the tunnel in Figure 7–9 means that one less person outside the tunnel can use the macrocell's capacity.

One of the fastest growing uses of repeaters is for in-building applications. In this situation, an antenna is placed on the roof of the building to transmit and receive mobile calls. The signal is then routed from the rooftop antenna, down through the building, to a small repeater on every floor. The signals from the repeater are transmitted and received through an antenna no bigger than a smoke alarm. With in-building repeaters, you can begin a cellular phone call in your car, continue it while you enter the building—even in the elevator—and finish it after you arrive at your desk. (There goes your last excuse to hang up on your mother-in-law.)

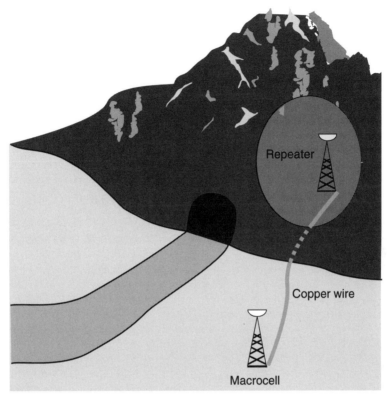

Figure 7–9   Graphical depiction of a repeater inside a tunnel.

Glossary

Absorption

Describes the process by which RF energy penetrates a material or substance and gets converted to heat. RF energy of the appropriate frequency will experience severe absorption when it encounters rain.

Adapter

A short, two-sided connector used to join connectors from different families. It is primarily used to connect a cable (with a connector from one family) to a cable or component (with a connector from a different family).

Air interface

A general term used to describe how a wireless signal interfaces with the free space between a cellular phone and a basestation. It usually involves modulating the RF carrier to increase the information carrying capacity of the wireless system. Examples include CDMA, TDMA, and FDMA.

Altimeter

A device which uses radar technology to determine an airplane's altitude by reflecting an RF signal off the ground.

Amplifier

An active RF component used to increase the power of an RF signal. Amplifiers come in three varieties: high power, low noise, and "other." Other includes variable gain amplifiers and limiting amplifiers. Amplifiers are mostly solid state today, but they can also be traveling wave tubes.

Amplitude modulation

A form of modulation which works by superimposing an information signal onto an RF carrier by varying the amplitude of successive sine waves of the carrier.

Analog

An electrical signal which varies over time and can take on any value between its minimum and maximum values.

Antenna

An RF component used to transform an RF signal, traveling on a conductor, into an airborne wave and vice versa. For antennas to work properly, their size must be similar to that of the wavelength of the signal they are intended to radiate. Antennas can be active or passive components.

Antenna pattern

A graphical tool used to show a birds-eye view of the RF energy radiating out from an antenna.

Attenuation

Phenomenon by which an RF signal is made smaller as it moves from one point to another. It is used interchangeably with the term insertion loss and it is measured in decibels.

Attenuator

An RF component used to make RF signals smaller by a predetermined amount, which is measured in decibels. There are two general categories of attenuators: fixed and variable. Fixed attenuators are also referred to as pads. There are two categories of variable attenuators: voltage variable attenuators and digital attenuators.

Balanced amplifier

An amplifier configuration which combines two amplifiers in parallel to provide redundancy and improved match.

Bandwidth

A measure of the usable frequency range of a component or application. It equals the difference between the upper frequency and the lower frequency and can be expressed in Hertz or as a percentage.

Baseband

The lowest frequency signal in a transmitter or receiver. It is the modulated RF signal after it is fully downconverted in a receiver or before it is upconverted in a transmitter.

Basestation

The wireless access point of a cellular system. It consists of all the necessary infrastructure to enable wireless communications including a tower, antennas, cables, RF transceivers, and power supplies. It is also referred to as a cell site.

Beamwidth

An angular measure, in degrees (of a circle), used to describe the width of the RF energy radiated from an antenna. It is also a measure of the width of an antenna pattern.

Bidirectional

Any RF component which works equally well in both directions. It can also be referred to as dual-directional. Antennas are almost always bi-directional while amplifiers are never so.

Broadband

Used to describe a characteristic of an RF component or wireless application with a "wide" bandwidth. It is also referred to as wideband. A rule of thumb is that any bandwidth greater than 50% is considered broadband.

Broadcasting

An RF system in which a single transmitter is used to communicate with a multitude of geographically dispersed receivers.

Cable assembly

A combination of bulk coaxial cable with coaxial connectors attached to each end.

Capacitor

A small, passive component used to shape electrical signals, found in every electrical circuit.

Carrier

An RF signal—ideally a perfect sine wave—which has an information signal superimposed upon it, through modulation, to carry it as a wave over the air.

Cavity

A family of RF components made by utilizing uniquely constructed hollow metal containers. Cavity components are primarily used for high power applications.

Cell site

See Basestations.

Cellular

A general term used to describe any one of several mobile wireless telephony applications which divide up a given geographical area into smaller subregions called cells.

Channel

A frequency subdivision of a bandwidth. Most RF applications divide their allocated bandwidth into different channels.

Circuit

An organized interconnection of passive and active electrical components to accomplish some electrical objective. A circuit can be further described as analog, digital, or RF, depending on the application.

Circulator

A three-port, passive RF device made of magnets and ferrite material which is used to control the direction of signal flow in an RF circuit.

Coaxial cable

Media used to transport an RF signal. It is comprised of an inner conductor (wire) surrounded by dielectric material (insulator) and covered by an outer conductor (shield). It is frequently referred to by its "RG" number.

Code division multiple access

A type of air interface which describes a technique of adding signal carrying capacity to a given bandwidth by allowing multiple signals to occupy the same frequency at the same time, and assigning each one the unique "address" of the intended receiver. It is also used to describe a form of direct sequence spread spectrum.

Collision avoidance

A radar system mounted on the front of an automobile which is used to determine the appropriate driving distance from the car in front. It is also used on airplanes.

Combiner

A passive RF device used to add together, in equal proportion, two or more RF signals.

Component

Any object an electrical signal encounters in a circuit. Used interchangeably with the term device, all components are either active or passive.

Connector

A cylindrical, metallic object firmly attached to a cable or component which is used to facilitate joining one to the other. It is also referred to as a coaxial connector.

Continuous wave

Any RF signal which is never turned off. It is primarily used to describe a type of radar in which the transmitter is always on.

Continuous wave radar

A type of radar in which the transmitted signal is always on. See also Doppler radar.

Conversion loss

The insertion loss a signal experiences in a mixer as it goes from the RF port to the IF port or vice versa. It is measured in decibels.

Coupler

A passive RF component in which the input signal is split unevenly and the smaller one is siphoned off to be used somewhere else in the system. This type of coupler can be directional or bidirectional. There is another type of coupler called a Lange or quadrature (or quad) coupler in which the signal is split evenly between two ports, but one of the outputs is phase-shifted from the other.

Quad couplers are also referred to as quad hybrids.

Current

Electrons on the move, either on a conductor or inside a component.

Decade

A bandwidth in which the highest frequency is 10 times bigger than the lowest frequency.

Decibel

A mathematical conversion, utilizing logarithms of a ratio, which is used as a unit of measure for RF signals. It is primarily used as a measure of the (power) gain and (insertion) loss of RF components.

Demodulation

The process of separating the RF carrier from the information signal in a modulated signal.

Demodulator

An RF device used to perform demodulation. It is a complex component which is comprised of active and passive devices, especially mixers.

Detector

A passive RF component used to convert an RF power signal into a voltage signal. It is used to supply a voltage, which is proportional to the RF power signal, to another component or piece of test equipment which is not designed to handle an RF power signal.

Device

See Component.

Dielectric

Any material which does not conduct electricity (an insulator). When used in the context of RF, dielectric material is a special type of insulator which is designed to minimize the insertion loss of an RF signal being carried on a conductor attached to it.

Digital

An electrical signal which varies over time and can take on only one of two values: high and low.

Digital signal processing

Describes the process of using sophisticated mathematical computations and signal processing to pack a lot of information into a digital signal.

Diode

A semiconductor device used in many RF components. There are several different types of RF diodes which are each manufactured differently to optimize different performance parameters.

Diplexer

See Duplexer.

Direct broadcast satellite

A high power, geosynchronous orbit satellite which transmits broadcast signals to be received by small antenna dishes attached to the home.

Direct sequence spread spectrum

A spread spectrum technique which involves "imprinting" a special digital code onto the RF carrier so that only the intended receiver can decipher it.

Directional coupler

A coupler which only works in one direction.

Discrete component

An electrical component which performs a single function and is housed in its own package.

Distributed circuit

A type of RF circuit philosophy in which some passive components are made from uniquely shaped circuit traces.

Divider

A passive RF device which equally divides an RF signal into two or more RF signals.

Doppler radar

A type of radar which utilizes the return signal's frequency shift to determine an object's velocity.

Downconverter

Another name for a mixer in a receiver; it is used to lower the frequency of the RF signal.

Downlink

The path an RF signal travels from a satellite to the ground.

Dual directional coupler

A coupler which works equally well in both directions.

Dual mode

Describes mobile phones which can communicate in both first generation cellular (analog) and second generation cellular (digital) modes.

Duplex

Describes an RF system which has the ability to transmit and receive simultaneously. Used most frequently with regard to telephony.

Duplexer

A passive RF device which contains two bandpass filters with different passbands. It is also called a diplexer.

Dynamic range

A measure of how large a signal an RF component can handle without distorting it. It is the key performance parameter of any device operating in a digital wireless system. One measure of a component's dynamic range is its third order intercept point, measured in dBm. Sometimes the dynamic range is specified as a combination of a component's third order intercept and its noise figure. The term is often used interchangeably with the term linearity.

Earth station

The name given to the ground facilities which communicate with a satellite.

Effective isotropic radiated power

Describes the amount of RF energy from a satellite which reaches the Earth within the satellite antenna's footprint.

Electronically scanned array

An antenna, made up of many small transceivers, which can sweep an antenna pattern without moving anything mechanically.

Feedback

An electrical circuit technique whereby a signal at one point in the system is sampled and "fed back" to a prior point in the system and used to make adjustments or corrections.

Ferrite

A composite material with excellent magnetic properties used to make isolators, circulators, and transformers.

Filter

A passive RF component which passes or rejects a signal solely on the basis of its frequency. There are four main categories of filters: low pass, high pass, bandpass, and band reject.

Fire control radar

A type of radar system, used in fighter aircraft, to control the targeting of a missile.

Footprint

The antenna pattern which the antenna on a satellite projects onto the Earth.

Frequency

The measure of how many complete sine wave cycles occur in one second in an RF signal, measured in Hertz.

Frequency division multiple access

A type of air interface which describes a technique of adding signal carrying capacity to a given bandwidth by dividing it up into smaller frequency bands.

Frequency hopping spread spectrum

A spread spectrum technique which involves constantly changing the RF carrier's frequency in such a way that only the intended receiver can decipher it.

Frequency modulation

A form of modulation which works by superimposing an information signal onto an

RF carrier by varying the frequency of successive sine waves of the carrier.

Frequency response

A graph of amplitude gain or loss, versus frequency, for an RF component. It is used to describe how the particular component behaves as the signal's frequency changes.

Frequency reuse

Describes the unique feature of mobile wireless telephone services in which more than one party can use the same exact frequency, at the same time, in a given geographical location.

Gain

The increase in size of the output signal of an amplifier with respect to the input signal. It is measured in decibels.

Gallium Arsenide

A compound semiconductor material, made of gallium and arsenic, used to make RF diodes and transistors. It is the preferred semiconductor material of choice for very high frequency RF products.

Geostationary orbit

See Geosynchronous orbit.

Geosynchronous orbit

An orbit, 22,000 miles above Earth, in which satellites rotate around the Earth at the same speed as the Earth's rotation, giving them the appearance of not moving.

Global positioning system

A system of 21 satellites which continuously transmit special signals used by special receivers to determine location.

Handoff

Describes the process whereby a mobile telephone call is transferred from one cell site to another with no interruption of service.

Hertz

The unit of measure for frequency, it measures a signal's "cycles per second."

Hybrid

When used in the context of circuit technologies, it describes an RF circuit made by combining chips and discrete components onto a ceramic substrate, which is also referred to as a microwave integrated circuit (MIC). When used in the context of coupling, it describes a Lange coupler.

Impedance

A measure of an RF component's input and output "size," expressed in ohms. In RF systems, the standard size used by all components is 50 ohms.

Impedance matching

The process of converting the output impedance of some RF device—which is not 50 ohms—to 50 ohms, so that it can be operatively connected to some other component.

Impedance ratio

A number used to quantify a transformer's ability to convert one impedance value to another. A transformer with a two-to-one (2:1) impedance ratio can convert a 100 ohm impedance to 50 ohms.

Inductor

A small, passive component used to shape electrical signals, made by winding a wire into a spiral. It is found in most electrical circuits.

Insertion loss

A measure of how much smaller the output signal of a passive device is with respect to the input signal. It is measured in decibels.

Insulator

Any material which does not conduct electricity.

Integrated circuit

Combining more than one active and/or passive device onto a single piece of semiconductor material.

Intercept point

See Third order intercept.

Intermediate frequency

The name of the signal between the two mixers in a two mixer receiver. It is also used to identify one of the ports of a mixer.

Isolation

A measure of the insertion loss in the "open" path of an RF switch, or between any two ports in a passive RF component. Like insertion loss, it is measured in decibels.

Isolator

A two-port passive RF device made of magnets and ferrite material which is used to protect other RF components from excessive signal reflection. Isolators are circulators in which the third port is connected to a heat dissipating load.

Lange coupler

See Coupler.

Limiting amplifier

An amplifier which is used to protect the RF device which comes after it by limiting its output power to a predetermined level, regardless of the input power.

Linearity

See Dynamic range.

Local loop

The telephone circuit from the home (or office) to the local telephone company and back.

Local multipoint distribution service

A fixed wireless application operating around 28 GHz which is ideally suited for wireless local loop service.

Local oscillator

An RF component which produces a perfect sine wave signal; it is connected to one of the ports of a mixer.

Loss

A measure of the decrease in size of an output signal from a passive component, with respect to the input signal. It is measured in decibels.

Lumped element circuit

A type of RF circuit philosophy which utilizes packaged passive components.

Macrocell

The family of cell sites with the greatest signal carrying capacity. They require relatively high power RF transmission.

Match

A measure of how perfectly two RF components "fit" together, which results in less of the RF signal between them being reflected.

Match is measured by VSWR, which is expressed as a ratio of X:1, and by return loss, which is measured in decibels.

Microcell

The family of cell sites which results from subdividing macrocells. They require a relatively moderate amount of transmitted RF power.

Microwave

A term loosely used to describe a range of frequencies between 1 and 40 GHz.

Microwave integrated circuit

See Hybrid.

Millimeter wave

A term loosely used to describe a range of frequencies greater than 40 GHz.

Mixer

A three-port RF component used to change the frequency of one of the input signals. It is sometimes referred to as an upconverter (in a transmitter) or a downconverter (in a receiver). Mixers can be active or passive devices, although most are passive.

Mobile switching center

The central communications hub of a cellular telephone system which is responsible for routing all the calls from the various basestations to other basestations or to the public switched telephone network, and for billing. It is also referred to as the mobile telephone switching office.

Mobile telephone switching office

See Mobile switching center.

Modulation

Superimposing an information signal onto an RF carrier by varying some aspect of the carrier. There are three fundamental types of modulation: amplitude modulation, phase modulation, and frequency modulation.

Modulator

A device which superimposes an information signal onto an RF carrier. It has two inputs (the carrier and the information signal) and one output (the modulated signal).

Monolithic microwave integrated circuit

An integrated circuit designed for RF purposes. It can be made of several different semiconductor materials, but the two most common are silicon and gallium arsenide.

Multipath

The phenomenon in which a single wireless signal takes two different paths to the intended receiver.

Narrowband

Used to describe a characteristic of an RF component or wireless application with a "narrow" bandwidth. A rule of thumb is that any bandwidth less than 50% is considered narrowband.

Noise

Any unwanted changes to an RF signal. Noise usually manifests itself as unwanted changes in the sine wave's amplitude, referred to as AM noise, although FM noise is also possible. Mixers are notorious for injecting noise onto an RF signal.

Noise figure

A measure of how much noise an RF component injects onto an RF signal. Noise figure, which is measured in decibels, is most often mentioned with regard to low noise amplifiers.

Octave

Describes a bandwidth in which the highest frequency is twice as big as the lowest frequency.

Omnidirectional

Describes an antenna which radiates RF energy out equally in all directions.

Oscillator

An active RF component with a sole purpose to produce a perfect sine wave at a predetermined frequency. It is also referred to as a source.

Pad

A fixed attenuator (its insertion loss is constant).

Passband

The frequency range of a bandpass filter which has low insertion loss and therefore allows the signal to pass. A passband is defined by identifying its upper and lower frequency.

Personal communication services

Second generation (digital) cellular services in the United States.

Phase locked loop

An oscillator which incorporates feedback in an effort to produce a more perfect sine wave. A phase locked loop can be part of a very sophisticated oscillator called a synthesizer.

Phase modulation

A form of modulation which works by superimposing an information signal onto an RF carrier by varying the phase of successive sine waves of the carrier.

Picocell

The smallest family of cell sites. They provide for the least signal-carrying capacity, cover the smallest area, and require the lowest amount of transmitted RF power.

Polarization

Refers to the fact that RF sine waves have spatial orientation to them as they travel in the air. The three types of polarization are horizontal, vertical, and circular.

Power divider

See Divider.

Printed circuit board

Describes a circuit technology in which metal traces are mounted on a plastic composite material which is used to interconnect electrical components. The motherboard inside a personal computer uses a printed circuit board.

Propagation delay

The time it takes for a signal to travel from the Earth to a satellite and back again. For satellites in geosynchronous orbit, the delay is about a quarter of a second.

Quadrature (Quad) coupler

See Coupler.

Quadrature (Quad) hybrid

See Coupler.

Radar

A wireless system which uses reflected RF energy to detect an object's range, location, and velocity.

Radar cross section

The effective area to reflect RF energy of a object being sensed by radar.

Radiate

A term used to describe the process by which an RF signal changes into an airborne wave.

Radio frequency

Shame on you. Used to identify a class of high frequency electrical signals intended to be radiated as waves. It is also used to describe a range of frequencies less than 1 GHz.

Receiver

One of the two main building blocks of a wireless system which is responsible for collecting the RF energy from the antenna and reducing the signal's frequency down to where it can be accepted by the demodulator.

Reflection

A term used to describe an RF signal's behavior when it encounters an impedance mismatch or a solid object. With an impedance mismatch, some (or all) of the RF energy is reflected back in the direction from which it came. With a solid object, the RF energy bounces off the object at the same angle at which it encountered it.

Repeater

A general term used to describe an RF system which is designed to geographically extend the RF coverage of a macrocell.

Resistor

A small, passive component used to reduce the size of electrical signals, it is found in every electrical circuit.

Return loss

A measure of match between two RF components, expressed in decibels. The better the match, the less energy reflected, the higher the return loss.

Saturation

The behavior of all amplifiers when the input power exceeds a certain point; the amplifier no longer amplifies and the output is more or less constant. When an amplifier is in the saturated region, it said to be nonlinear and causes distortion to the RF signal.

Scanning

Electrically or mechanically moving a radar's antenna pattern to achieve radar coverage over a large area.

Self-resonant frequency

The frequency at which an object will oscillate if sufficiently excited by electrical energy. Almost all solid objects have a self-resonant frequency.

Signal

Electrical energy which is made to vary, over time, in a controlled manner.

Silicon

A semiconductor material used to make RF diodes and transistors. Because it is low cost, it is the preferred material choice for low frequency RF products.

Skin effect

A term used to describe an RF signal's behavior when it is on a conductor. Because of their high frequency, RF signals do not penetrate into solid conductors, but rather exist exclusively on the outer surface.

Source

See Oscillator.

Specialized mobile radio

A cellularlike service in the United States which combines standard cellular operation with dispatch capability.

Spectrum

A term used to describe a range of frequencies for a specific application.

Spread spectrum

A digital modulation scheme which increases the signal carrying capacity of a given bandwidth by allowing multiple signals to occupy the same frequency and distinguishing each one by its unique "address." The modulation process causes each signal's bandwidth to increase.

Station keeping

The practice, by satellites, of using small bursts of propellant to change position to ensure that they do not stray very far from their intended location in geosynchronous orbit.

Stopband

The frequency range of a band reject filter which has high insertion loss and therefore stops signals from passing. A stopband is defined by identifying its upper and lower frequency.

Subassembly

See subsystem.

Subsystem

An RF item, in a single container, which performs more than one function and utilizes more than one component. For example, a combination of a mixer, a filter and an amplifier in a single box is considered a subsystem.

Surface acoustic wave

An electrical signal converted to a sound wave. In surface acoustic wave devices, the sound wave travels along the surface of the device, rather than inside of it.

Switch

An active RF component which switches a single input between one or more outputs. RF switches are characterized by their number of poles (switches) and throws (outputs).

Synthesizer

A very sophisticated oscillator incorporating other electronic circuitry, plus feedback, to make a more perfect sine wave.

T/R switch

A single-pole, double-throw switch situated between a transmitter, a receiver, and an antenna.

Thermal impedance

A measure of how hot a component gets for a given amount of power dissipated. It is expressed in °C/watt.

Third order intercept

The measure of an RF component's linearity or dynamic range, expressed in dBm. It is also referred to as the intercept point. The higher the measure, the more linear the component and the less distortion of the RF signal.

Time division multiple access

A type of air interface which describes a technique of adding signal carrying capacity by breaking up each frequency allocation into multiple time slots and assigning each signal a specific slot.

Trace

A small, thin piece of metal on a dielectric material used to carry signals.

Transceiver

A combination transmitter and receiver in a single package.

Transfer curve

A graph of output power versus input power of an amplifier.

Transformer

A passive RF component used in impedance matching, among other things. It is defined by its impedance ratio.

Transistor

A semiconductor device utilized primarily in amplifiers to create gain; they can also be used by other RF components to perform switching. There are many different varieties of transistors which are made from different semiconductor materials.

Transmitter

One of the two main building blocks in a wireless system which is responsible for taking the signal from the modulator, increasing its frequency and power, then radiating it out the antenna.

Transponder

An RF subsystem onboard a satellite which is responsible for receiving the uplink signal, converting it to the downlink frequency, and then retransmitting it.

Traveling wave tube

An older technology RF amplifier which amplifies RF signals in a vacuum, inside a cavity.

Triangulation

A method for determining position by receiving three different wireless signals from three different locations.

Triplexer

A passive RF device which contains three bandpass filters with different passbands.

Tuner

An RF device, used in a receiver, to frequency-select individual channels.

Upconverter

Another name for a mixer used in a transmitter which is used to raise the frequency of the RF signal.

Uplink

The path an RF signal travels from the ground to a satellite.

Varactor

A diode used to vary the frequency in a voltage-controlled oscillator.

Variable gain amplifier

An amplifier with an external control which is used to vary its gain.

Very small aperture terminal

An RF system in which many small Earth stations use a satellite to communicate with a single receiver.

Voltage

Electrical potential. There are two types: AC (alternating), like the kind in a wall outlet, and DC (direct), like the kind in a battery.

Voltage-controlled oscillator

An oscillator with an external control which is used to vary its output frequency.

Voltage standing wave ratio

A measure of match between two RF components, expressed as a ratio of X:1. The lower the X, the better the match.

Watts

Unit of measure for any kind of power, e.g., RF, heat, etc.

Waveguide

Pipes, with rectangular cross sections, used to carry RF signals from one point to another. Inside, the RF signals move as waves and the waveguide serves to guide and control their movement.

Wavelength

A measure of the length of an RF signal. The higher a signal's frequency, the shorter its wavelength.

Wideband

See broadband.

Wireless

A marketing term generally used to describe the newer RF applications.

Wireless local area networks

A local area network of computers which communicate via wireless signals.

Wireless local loop

An RF system which allows wireless communication with the local telephone company.

Appendix A–
Acronyms

This appendix includes the most commonly used acronyms in the RF and wireless industry. Some of the more arcane acronyms have been omitted because they do not experience widespread use. Because of the nature of the wireless industry, this list will almost certainly be incomplete. (The darn engineers can abbreviate things faster than publishers can publish.)

AC   *Alternating current,* power from a wall outlet.

AGC   *Automatic gain control,* control of a variable gain amplifier.

AM   *Amplitude modulation*, a type of modulation.

AMPS   *Advanced mobile phone service,* first generation cellular in the United States.

ASIC   *Application-specific integrated circuit,* a custom integrated circuit.

BASK   *Binary amplitude shift keying*, digital amplitude modulation.

BER   *Bit error rate,* the number of errors per second in a transmitted signal.

BPF   *Bandpass filter,* a type of filter.

BPSK   *Bi-phase shift keying*, a type of phase modulation.

BTA   *Basic trading area,* a small geographical area allocated for PCS.

CDMA   *Code division multiple access,* spread spectrum for mobile phones.

CDPD   *Cellular digital packet data,* wireless data communication using cellular phones.

CL   *Conversion loss,* the insertion loss of a mixer.

CW   *Continuous wave,* an RF system in which the transmitter is always on.

D-AMPS   *Digital AMPS,* a digital version of AMPS.

dB   *Decibels,* a relative measure of signal strength.

DBS   *Direct broadcast satellite,* TV signals from satellites direct to the home.

DC   *Direct current,* power from a battery.

DCS   *Digital communication services,* second generation cellular in Europe.

DGPS   *Differential GPS,* more accurate GPS.

DPDT   *Double-pole double-throw,* a type of RF switch.

DQPSK   *Differential quadrature phase shift keying,* a type of phase modulation.

DRO   *Dielectric resonator oscillator,* a type of oscillator.

DSP   *Digital signal processing* (or *processor),* a type of electrical signal processing.

DSSS   *Direct sequence spread spectrum,* a type of spread spectrum.

DTO   *Dielectrically tuned oscillator,* a variable DRO.

EIRP   *Effective isotropic radiated power,* the power radiated from a satellite's antenna.

EMC   *Electromagnetic compatibility,* acceptable levels of EMI.

EMI   *Electromagnetic interference,* a type of RF noise.

FCC   *Federal Communications Commission,* U.S government airwaves regulators.

FDMA   *Frequency division multiple access,* breaks up conversations by frequency.

FHSS   *Frequency hopping spread spectrum,* a type of spread spectrum.

FM   *Frequency modulation,* a type of modulation.

GaAs   *Gallium arsenide,* a type of semiconductor material.

GEO   *Geosynchronous orbit,* 22,000 miles above Earth.

GMSK   *Gaussian minimum shift keying,* a type of phase modulation.

GPS   *Global positioning system,* a satellite constellation used to determine location.

GSM   *Group special mobile,* a popular cellular standard in Europe.

HBT   *Heterojunction bipolar transistor,* a new type of fast transistor.

HDTV   *High definition television,* next generation digital TV.

HEMT   *High electron mobility transistor,* a very high frequency transistor.

HF   *High frequency,* frequency between 3 and 30 MHz.

HPA   *High power amplifier,* a type of amplifier used at the output of a transmitter.

HPF   *High pass filter,* a type of filter.

Hz   *Hertz,* the measure of a signal's frequency in cycles per second.

IC   *Integrated circuit,* multiple electrical components on a single semiconductor.

IF   *Intermediate frequency,* one of the signals used by a mixer.

IL   *Insertion loss,* the loss a signal experiences in a passive component.

IMD   *Intermodulation distortion,* a type of RF signal noise.

IMT   *International mobile telephone,* third generation cellular.

ISM   *Industrial, Scientific, Medical,* a family of frequency allocations for such use.

ITU   *International Telecommunications Union,* the FCC for the world.

JTACS   *Japan TACS,* Japanese version of TACS.

LAN   *Local area network,* computers hooked together.

LCC   *Leadless chip carrier,* a type of RF component package.

LDMOS   *Laterally diffused metal oxide semiconductor,* a type of transistor.

LEO   *Low Earth orbit,* a few hundred miles above Earth.

LHC   *Left hand circular,* a type of polarization.

LMDS   *Local multipoint distribution service,* a high frequency fixed wireless service.

LMR   *Land mobile radio,* a wireless application.

LNA   *Low noise amplifier*, a type of amplifier used at the input of a receiver.

LNB   *Low noise block converter*, an LNA and a mixer in the same package.

LO   *Local oscillator*, one of the inputs to a mixer.

LPF   *Low pass filter*, a type of filter.

LTCC   *Low temperature cofired ceramic*, a multilayer MIC circuit.

MCM   *Multichip module*, an RF subsystem hybrid.

MCPA   *Multicarrier power amplifier*, a type of very linear power amplifier.

MESFET *Metal semiconductor field effect transistor*, a high frequency transistor.

MIC   *Microwave integrated circuit*, a particular circuit technology.

MMIC   *Monolithic microwave integrated circuit*, an RF integrated circuit.

MOSFET *Metal oxide semiconductor field effect transistor*, a low frequency transistor.

MSA   *Metropolitan statistical area*, an urban geographical area allocated to cellular.

MSC   *Mobile switching center*, the brains of the cellular system.

MSK   *Minimum shift keying*, a type of phase modulation.

MTA   *Metropolitan trading area*, a large geographical area allocated for PCS.

MTSO   *Mobile telephone switching office*, the brains of the cellular system.

NADC   *North American digital cellular*, a digital cellular standard.

NF   *Noise figure*, the measure of quietness of an LNA.

NMT   *Nordic mobile telephone*, a cellular standard used in Scandinavian countries.

NODS   *Near object detection system*, a radar system for the rear bumper of a car.

OCXO   *Oven-controlled crystal oscillator*, a type of oscillator.

OEM   *Original equipment manufacturer*, a manufacturer.

PA   *Power amplifier*, same as HPA.

PAE	*Power added efficiency,* a measure of a power amplifier's efficiency.
PCB	*Printed circuit board,* a particular circuit technology.
PCN	*Personal communications network,* a new wireless application.
PCS	*Personal communication services,* second generation cellular in the United States.
PDC	*Personal digital cellular,* a Japanese cellular standard.
PHEMT	*Pseudomorphic high electron mobility transistor,* a very high frequency transistor.
PLL	*Phase locked loop,* a feedback technique used in an oscillator.
PLO	*Phase locked oscillator,* an oscillator which utilizes a PLL.
PM	*Phase modulation,* a type of modulation.
PSTN	*Public switched telephone network,* the local phone company.
QAM	*Quadrature amplitude modulation,* a type of complex modulation.
QPSK	*Quadrature phase shift keying,* a type of phase modulation.
RBOC	*Regional Bell operating company,* the baby Bells.
RF	*Radio frequency,* shame on you.
RFI	*Radio frequency interference,* unwanted RF signals.
RFIC	*Radio frequency integrated circuit,* self explanatory.
RHC	*Right hand circular,* a type of polarization.
RSA	*Rural statistical area,* a rural geographical area allocated for cellular.
SAW	*Surface acoustic wave,* an electrical signal as a sound wave.
Si	*Silicon,* a type of semiconductor material.
SMR	*Specialized mobile radio,* a cellularlike mobile phone service.
SMT	*Surface mount technology,* a method of mounting components on a PCB.
SPDT	*Single-pole double-throw,* a type of switch.
SPST	*Single-pole single-throw,* a type of switch.
SSPA	*Solid state power amplifier,* a power amplifier made from transistors.
TACS	*Total access communications systems,* similar to AMPS.
TCXO	*Temperature controlled crystal oscillator,* a type of oscillator.

TDMA   *Time division multiple access,* breaking up signals into multiple time slots.

TWT   *Traveling wave tube,* a type of RF amplifier.

TWTA   *Traveling wave tube amplifier,* same as a TWT.

UHF   *Ultra high frequency,* frequency between 300 MHz and 3 GHz.

VCO   *Voltage-controlled oscillator,* a type of oscillator.

VCXO   *Voltage-controlled crystal oscillator,* a type of oscillator.

VGA   *Variable gain amplifier,* a type of amplifier.

VHF   *Very high frequency,* frequency between 30 and 300 MHz.

VSAT   *Very small aperture terminal,* a multipoint-to-point satellite system.

VSWR   *Voltage standing wave ratio,* the measure of a component's match.

VTO   *Voltage tuned oscillator,* same as VCO.

VVA   *Voltage variable attenuator,* an attenuator whose attenuation can vary.

WCDMA   *Wideband CDMA,* CDMA used for PCS telephony.

WLAN   *Wireless local area network,* computers connected without wires.

WLL   *Wireless local loop,* wireless local telephone service.

YIG   *Yttrium-Iron-Garnet,* an alloy used in oscillators.

Appendix B–
Specifications

This appendix is intended for people working in the RF industry who need to understand the arcane language of component performance. Contained herein are the most common electrical performance characteristics of RF components. Each parameter is broken down by its specification name, its most common symbol or acronym, the unit of measure, and where it is most often used.

Specification	Symbol or Acronym	Unit of measure	Typically measures
Amplitude unbalance		dB	The difference in insertion loss on two paths of a power divider.
Attenuation		dB	The amount of signal loss in an attenuator or other passive component.
Bandwidth	BW	MHz, GHz	The useful frequency range of a component.
Compression point (output)	P_1dB	dBm	The linear power output capability of a component.
Compression point (input)		dBm	The linear power input capability of a component.

Specification	Symbol or Acronym	Unit of measure	Typically measures
Conversion gain		dB	The signal gain in an active mixer.
Conversion loss	CL	dB	The insertion loss in a passive mixer.
Coupling		dB	The amount of the signal which is "siphoned off" in a directional coupler.
Directivity		dB	The ability of a directional coupler to direct RF energy onto the desired port.
Gain	G	dB	The amount a signal increases as it passes through an amplifier.
Gain flatness	ΔG	dB	How much the gain of an amplifier varies over its bandwidth.
Harmonics (suppression)		dBc	The amount of unwanted signals, in a particular bandwidth, which are a frequency multiple of the desired signal.
Image rejection		dB	The amount of attenuation of the unwanted signal coming out of a mixer.
Impedance	Ω	ohms	The resistance a signal experiences when entering a component.
Impedance ratio	N:1		The impedance changing ability of a transformer.
Insertion loss	IL	dB	The loss a signal experiences as it travels through a passive component.
Intermodulation distortion	IMD	dBc	The amount of unwanted signals as a result of mixing two signals.
Isolation	ISOL	dB	The insertion loss in the open path of a switch or between two ports on a passive device.

Specification	Symbol or Acronym	Unit of measure	Typically measures
Match	VSWR		How well a signal is transferred from one component to another.
Noise figure	NF	dB	The input sensitivity of a low noise amplifier.
Noise temperature		°K	The input sensitivity of very low noise figure LNAs.
Phase noise		dBc/Hz	Signal distortion resulting from unintended phase modulation.
Phase shift	$\Delta\phi$	degrees	The angular shift in an RF signal as it travels through a component.
Phase unbalance		degrees	The difference in phase shift on two paths of a power divider.
Power added efficiency	PAE	%	The efficiency with which a power amplifier turns DC power into RF power.
Pulling factor		MHz	The change in the output frequency of an oscillator when the input impedance of the device it is driving changes.
Return loss	RL	dB	The amount of the signal which is reflected at the interface of two components.
Reverse isolation	S_{12}	dB	The isolation from the output to the input of a component.
Saturated power	Psat	dBm	The maximum amount of power an amplifier can put out.
Second order intercept	Ip2	dBm	The linearity of a component.
Selectivity	Q		The efficiency of a filter in tuning out unwanted frequencies.

Specification	Symbol or Acronym	Unit of measure	Typically measures
Settling time		msec	The time it takes for a VCO's output to stabilize after a frequency change.
Spurious noise (spurs)		dBc	Random noise in an RF signal.
Stability		ppm	The change in output frequency of an oscillator over time.
Switching time	tsw	msec, nsec	The time for a switch to change positions.
Thermal impedance	θjc	°C/W	The rise in temperature of a component which is dissipating power.
Third order intercept (output)	Ip3, OIP	dBm	The linearity of a component's output signal.
Third order intercept (input)	IIP	dBm	The linearity of a component's input signal.
Tuning sensitivity		MHz/V	The change in the output frequency of a VCO with a change in the control voltage.

Bibliography

Chang, Kai, *Handbook of Microwave and Optical Components, Volume 1*, John Wiley & Sons, NY, 1989.

Cheung, Stephen W., and Levien, Frederic H., *Microwaves Made Simple*, Artech House, MA, 1985.

Danzer, Paul, *The Arrl Handbook for Radio Amateurs*, American Radio Relay League, 1999.

Elbert, Bruce R., *Introduction to Satellite Communications,* Artech House, MA, 1987.

Hurn, Jeff, *GPS, A Guide to the Next Utility,* Trimble Navigation, CA, 1989.

Lebow, Irwin, *Information Highways & Byways*, IEEE Press, New York, 1995.

Nellist, John G., *Understanding Telecommunications and Lightwave Systems*, IEEE Press, New York, 1992.

Smith, Clint, *Practical Cellular & PCS Design*, McGraw-Hill, New York, 1998.

Stimson, George W., *Introduction to Airborne Radar*, Hughes Aircraft Co.,
     1983.

Synergy, *Designer's Handbook*, Synergy Microwave, 1999.

About the Author

Carl Weisman attended the Pennsylvania State University where he earned a BSEE in 1980. From there he went to work for the Hughes Aircraft Company as a design engineer working on airborne radar for fighter aircraft. During his nine-year stay there, he was awarded a Hughes Fellowship which enabled him to earn an MSEE from the University of Southern California while working full time.

Mr. Weisman spent the next eight years working in sales and the marketing of RF and wireless hardware for several companies including Avantek-Hewlett Packard and M/A-COM-AMP. During this period he spent a great deal of time conducting product training for non-technical salespeople in the industry, which served as the inspiration for this book.

Mr. Weisman recently earned his MBA from Loyola Marymount University where he graduated with honors. He currently spends his time working on other writing projects and pursuing entrepreneurial opportunities. Mr. Weisman lives in Redondo Beach, CA, and can be reached at weisman@flash.net.

Index